- *THIS IS THE THIRD ISSUE OF* -

Buckman Journal

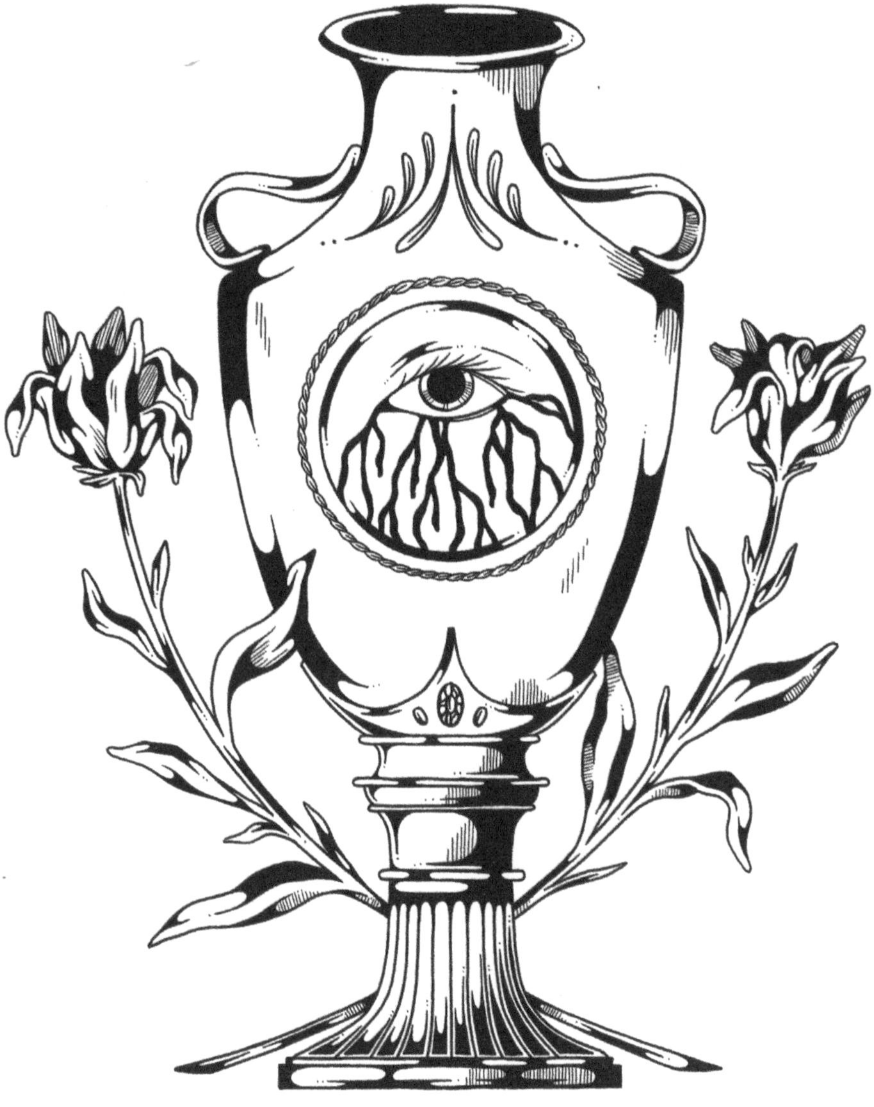

Portland, OR

Buckmanjournal.com | Buckman Publishing, LLC

THE BUCKMAN TEAM IS

Editor
Jerry Sampson

Art Director
Ellen Robinette

Journal Design
Jodie Beechem

Operations Manager
Emmi Greer

Scout
Liz Lampman

Social Media Assist and Scout:
Sarah Kue

Art Gallery Assist
One Grand Gallery

ISBN 978-1-7337245-0-0

CONTENTS

Letter From The Editor	2	
Artwork Contributors	4	
Space Traitors by Walidah Imarisha	9	Artwork by Jeremy Okai Davis
Wild Buffaloes by Justin Hocking	17	Artwork by Sean Croghan
Missed Connections #2 by Joel Preston Smith	20	Artwork by Brianna Spencer
Ghosted by Susan DeFreitas	23	Artwork by Shannon O'Connor
	32	Artwork & Poetry by Alyson Provax
Undergrowth by Miranda Schmidt	35	Artwork by Aaron Wessling
Missed Connections #6 by Joel Preston Smith	42	Artwork by Brianna Spencer
Made by Brutal Breasts by Craig Buchner	45	Artwork by Leslie Dorcus
	56	Artwork & Poetry by Alyson Provax
Final Call From Portland Meadows by Rich Perin	59	Artwork by Hattie Watson
Torso Wall by Joe Galván	69	Artwork by Allynn Carpenter
	78	Artwork & Poetry by Alyson Provax
Strings and Sealing Wax by Arlo Voorhees	81	Artwork by Zachary Schomburg
Missed Connections #12 by Joel Preston Smith	86	Artwork by Brianna Spencer
Racing Josephine by Tammy Stoner	89	Artwork by Amanda Jackson
Interview with Lauren Prado by Jess Andra	99	Artwork by Lauren Prado
The Deer Mother by Francesca G. Varela	107	Artwork by Rachel Sabin
Missed Connections #19 by Joel Preston Smith	118	Artwork by Brianna Spencer
	120	Artwork & Poetry by Alyson Provax
They Come from the Void by Luke Elliott	123	Artwork by Mike Vos
Missed Connections #22 by Joel Preston Smith	134	Artwork by Brianna Spencer

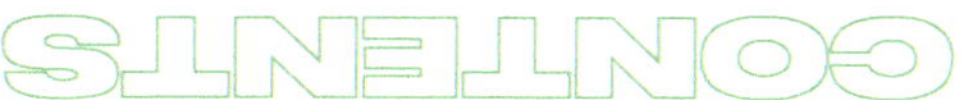

LETTER FROM THE EDITOR

'm having a nightmare.

In it, the world has taken the blueish hue of a computer screen. I walk by a stranger and he reaches out and swipes his finger across my forehead. Before I can react, my body is lifted by invisible hands and tossed off the sidewalk–to the left. The man snickers and flips me the bird. I stand up, shaking, and dip into the open door of a brightly lit storefront.

Inside, hundreds of people are standing nose-to-nose, screaming at one another with a vitriol that terrifies me. At once, everyone turns to me, pointing, mouths wide open, eyes glassy and filled with hunger. I can't move. I can't scream.

I wake up, thank Jeeves, and lift my head from the keyboard. My face sticks to the keys and makes the unnerving sound of skin peeling from plastic.

My dreamscape lingers in the blue light of my laptop. I question reality. Siri asks me if I'm alright. I assure her I'm fine.

+++++

BUCKMAN JOURNAL ISSUE 003 EXPLORES THE WAY TECHNOLOGY AND MEDIA WORKS WITH, FOR AND AGAINST, OUR WORLD.

• In **Space Traitors**, a man awakens to a new world as Obama is elected president, and aliens invade.

• **Wild Buffaloes** features an intense interview with an immigrant, showing the dark side of the truth beyond the Wall.

• Finding a note tucked into the folds of a book catapults a heartbroken woman into a dreamlike affair in **Ghosted**.

• Immersing themselves in the deep woods for a weekend camping trip, the grieving couple in **Undergrowth** are confronted by dangers within the forest, and can no longer avoid their darkest fears, or one another.

• Clutching onto the dream of meeting the right person, **The Missed Connections** toss their luck into the void and hope to reach the ones they're looking for.

• **Made by Brutal Beasts** confronts the furry implications of impending fatherhood.

• In **Final Call at the Portland Meadows** we take one last look at a city landmark before saying goodbye for good and all.

• After a sexy night with an online hookup, Justin Chu realizes that not everything on Grindr is what it seems. In fact...is anything on the **Torso Wall** what it seems?

• In this world of streaming platforms and throwaway pop stars, **Strings and Sealing Wax** explores the nature of our relationship to music and how it has changed as technology progresses.

• Living a life of regret and guilt causes the aimless woman in **Racing Josephine** to be unable to stay in one place, with memories that haunt, and can't be erased by the bottle.

• In **The Deer Mother**, two women connect despite desperately seeking solitude.

• **They Come From the Void** delves into the mystery and cosmic horror of a small town that has been blessed – or cursed – with a collection of god-like alien orbs. ◗

ARTWORK CONTRIBUTORS

AARON WESSLING

Aaron Wessling is a Portland-based photographer and a co-founder of The Portland Darkroom. His work, shot primarily on medium format color negative film, explores themes of impermanence, memory, and longing. Aaron's work has been featured at Newspace Center for Photography and LightBox Photographic Gallery, and his series "Close" is currently on display in the Pacific Northwest Photography Viewing Drawers at Blue Sky Gallery. *(pg. 34)*

insta: @aaronwessling

AMANDA JACKSON

Portland resident and artist Mandie Jackson uses photography to blend whimsical elements and unusual color palettes to create portraits that celebrate the beauty of femininity while challenging the conventional ways in which we see the world. *(pg. 88)*

insta: @mandie_mannequin

SHANNON O'CONNOR

Shannon O'Connor is originally from Los Angeles, born in 1986, and moved to Oregon in 2014. She is a photographer, filmmaker, collage artist, curator and gallery owner. Her photography and collage work explores the translation of her intuition into visual images. Shannon also creates video documentaries about artists, exploring their personal stories and creative processes. She studied commercial photography at Santa Monica College and currently works as a freelance photographer and curator. Additionally, she was the director of Bleicher Project Space in Los Angeles from 2011-2012, and currently Co-owns Wolff Gallery in Portland, OR since 2015. *(pg. 22)*

insta: @shannonphotograph

BRIANNA SPENCER

Brianna Spencer is on a noodle flying through the air, she wiggles in and out of art consciousness and displays work in areas like San Diego and Portland OR. She loves the kids books of her childhood, and silly little drawings that embody her ideal state, silliness. The noodle flys and she flys with it. *(pg. 21, 43, 87, 116, 133)*

insta: @freckledbee

ARTWORK CONTRIBUTORS

ZACHARY SCHOMBURG

Zachary Schomburg is responsible for one novel, Mammother (Featherproof Books 2017) and 5 books of poems including, most recently, Pulver Maar (Black Ocean, 2019). He is also an illustrator, muralist, teacher, and the publisher of an independent poetry press called Octopus Books. He still lives in Portland, OR. *(pg. 80)*

zacharyschomburg.net

insta: @zacharyschomburg

JEREMY OKAI DAVIS

Jeremy Okai Davis has lived in Portland since 2007. His illustrations appear in American Songwriter Magazine, while his art has featured in galleries across the nation, including The Studio Museum of Harlem in New York City. Permanent installations of his work can be found at the Lonnie B. Harries Black Cultural Center at Oregon State University, as well as six large scale paintings in the University of Oregon's Allen Hall. *(pg. 8)*

insta: @jeremyokaiart

LESLIE DORCUS

Leslie Dorcus is a printmaker living in Portland, Oregon. They received their BFA in Printmaking at the Rhode Island School of Design (RISD) in 2011. They are an active member of Flight-64, a member run non-profit print studio.

In their work they create narrative landscapes and abstract self portraits using a language of symbols and patterns. The obsessively reoccurring symbolic images explore the loops and repetitive nature of the residue of traumatic experience and OCD coping mechanisms. It is a therapeutic way of biting back and reclaiming their sense of self. *(pg. 44)*

lesliedorcus.weebly.com

insta: @tender_enemies

HATTIE WATSON

Hattie Watson is a photographer and world traveler based in Portland, Oregon. *(pg. 58-67)*

hattiewatson.com

insta: @hattiewatson

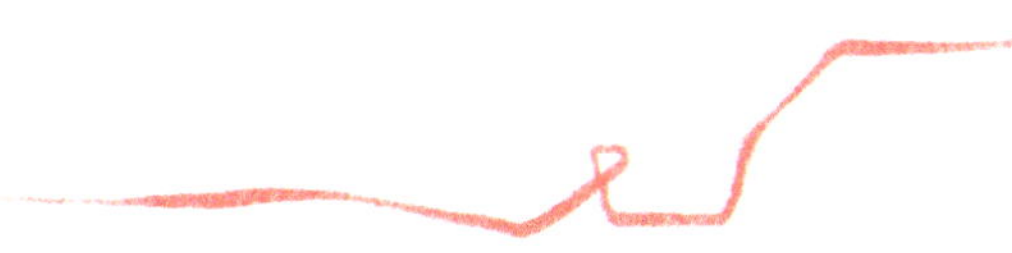

ARTWORK CONTRIBUTORS

MIKE VOS

Mike Vos is a Portland based, self-taught large format film photographer. Vos is also a musician, DJ, social worker and skateboarding instructor. He moved to PDX in 2004 yet continues to travel extensively for his various creative projects. He has shared his music and art across the U.S., Canada, Australia, Japan and Europe.

His passions have brought him into contact with numerous cultures, lifestyles and landscapes, where he draws deeply from for his photographic installations and artistic vision. He's world renowned for his commitment to environmental justice through the wide spectrum of artistic expression. His work posits a world without humans and explores the regrowth of the natural world amidst industrial decay. *(pg. 120)*
insta: @deadcitiesphoto

TYLER BINGHAM

Awake is a psychedelic abstract artist living in Portland, OR. Using gouache, acrylic paint pen, and ink his art is expressive and personal. *(cover)*
insta: @awake_pdx

SEAN CROGHAN

Sean Croghan is an artist & musician residing in and from Portland, Oregon. Best known for his bands Crackerbash and The Pynnacles, Croghan began painting in order to tell stories by a different means and has since had several solo shows related to his love of the PNW, mythology, and to his life here. *(pg. 16)*
insta: @sdcroghan

ALYSON PROVAX

Alyson Provax is an artist interested in language, feelings, and memory. Her practice is grounded in printmaking, and she often uses non-traditional methods of letterpress resulting in solo pieces, animations, and public works rather than printed editions. She has shown regionally at Wolff Gallery, Upfor Gallery, Bridge Productions, The Vestibule and the Whatcom Museum, nationally at A.I.R. Gallery and The Untitled Space in New York, and internationally at the Blueproject Foundation in Barcelona. Her work appeared in articles about artists' responses to the 2016 election in New York Magazine, Newsweek and ArtSlant. In June 2019 her work appeared on billboards and bus benches in Portland for something nameless, which was funded in part by a grant from the Regional Arts and Culture Council. *(pg. 32, 56, 118, foldout)*
insta: @alysonprovax

ARTWORK CONTRIBUTORS

RACHEL SABIN

Portland-based artist Rachel Sabin was born and raised in Oregon; the state's scenic beauty holds a direct influence on her most recent series of oil paintings, "Liminal Deities." Based on reflection photos she takes while kayaking, these canvases offer a glimpse into texture-filled borderlands where elemental gods and unknown creatures emerge. The shoreline is rotated, highlighting abstract patterns that gain faces and identities under the viewer's gaze. Rachel has been working with oil paint since 2009, when she won an independent research grant at her alma mater, Willamette University. Additional work can be seen at www.rachelsabin.com *(pg. 104)*

insta: @paintsabin

LAUREN PRADO

Born and raised in sunny California, Lauren Prado spends most of her free time sewing in 80 degree weather. Prado uses fiber, yarn, and needles to create representations of the digital images/products that flood our online feeds. Prado was a high school teacher for three years, and that experience largely influenced her interest in pop culture and the millennial lifestyle that centers on technology, online presence, and self-presentation. *(pg. 98, 101, 102)*

ALLYNN CARPENTER

Allynn Carpenter is an artist living and working in Portland, Oregon. He works in oil painting, colored pencil, guauche, photography, and collage. Allynn's primary area of interest is the body. His own transition as a transgender man has influenced how he perceives the relationship between the body and personal identity. Working with themes of transformation, gender, and the complexities of self-image, he assembles intimate self portraits that incorporate guauche, colored pencil, and photos of his own body.

Allynn got his MFA in Visual Studies at The Pacific Northwest College of Art. He has shown work throughout the Pacific Northwest. *(pg. 68)*

insta: @allynn_art

JODIE BEECHEM

Jodie is an illustrator, designer, and Oregonian, with a work ethic to match. She is constantly inspired by science fiction, art history, and anything remotely spooky. When she's not being creative, she's usually either watching live music or at an arcade playing pinball.

jodiebeechem.com

insta: @jodiebeechem

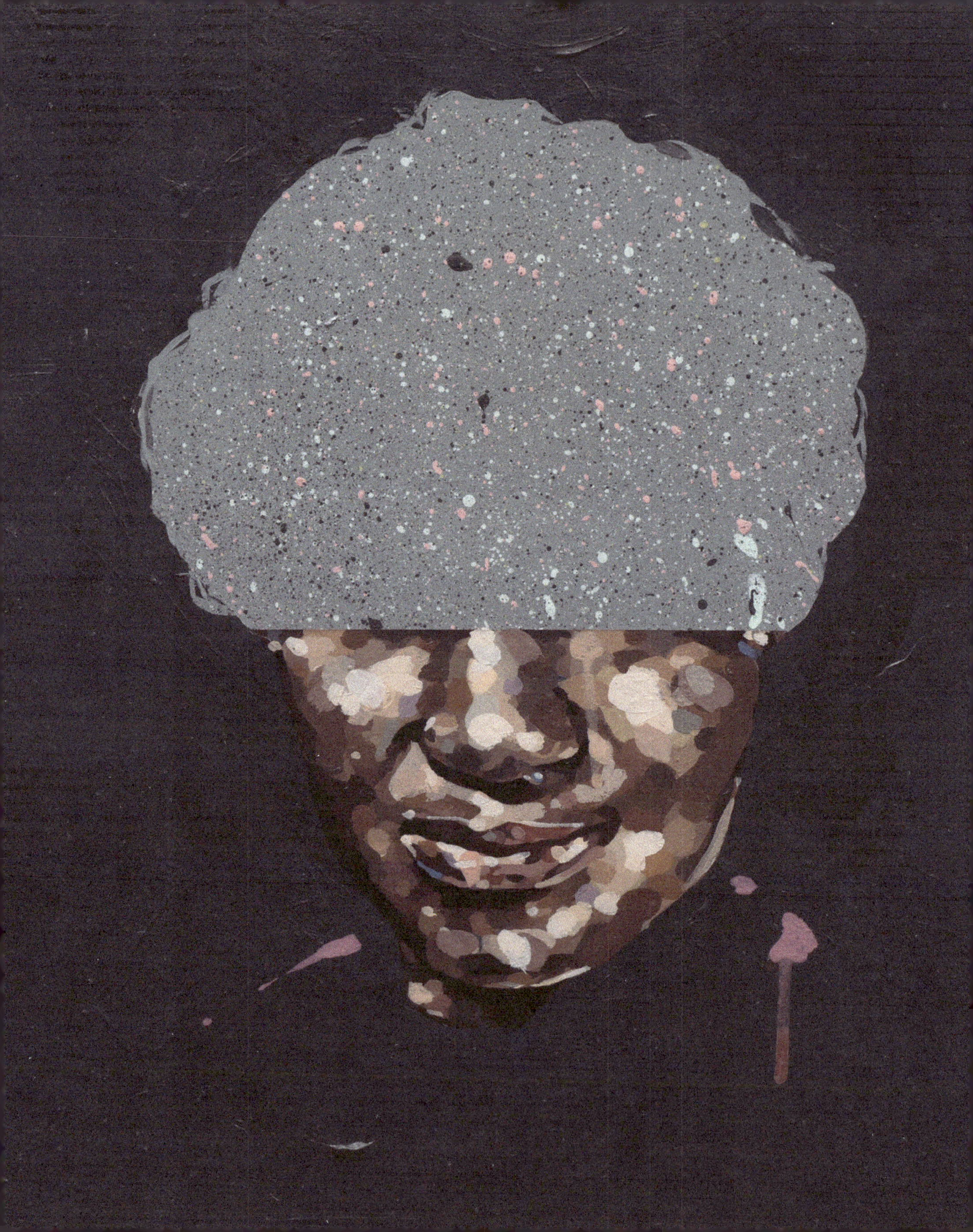

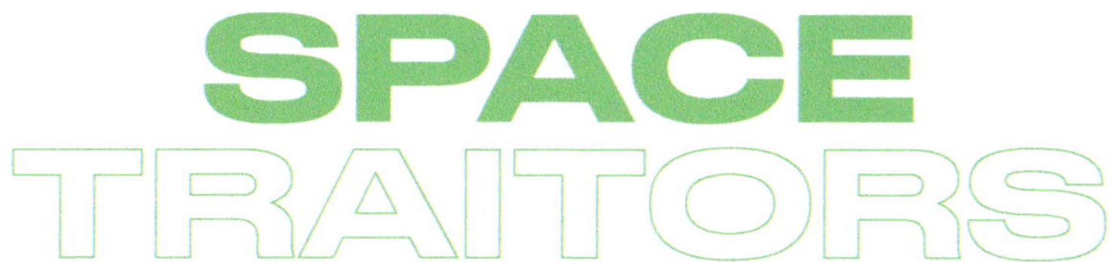

In conversation with Derrick Bell's
short story "Space Traders"

Words by Walidah Imarisha
Artwork by Jeremy Okai Davis

Walidah Imarisha is an educator, writer, public scholar, and poet. Co-editor of two anthologies including *Octavia's Brood: Science Fiction Stories From Social Justice Movements,* Imarisha also authored *Angels with Dirty Faces: Three Stories of Crime, Prison and Redemption,* winner of a 2017 Oregon Book Award, and the poetry collection *Scars/Stars.* In 2015, she received a Tiptree Fellowship for her science fiction writing. She spent 6 years with Oregon Humanities' Conversation Project as a public scholar facilitating programs across the state about Oregon Black history and other topics. Imarisha has taught at Stanford University, Pacific Northwest College of the Arts, Portland State University, and Oregon State University.

The trilling of the phone was almost equal to the pounding in Jamar's head. He reached out his hand without bothering to open his eyes, groping blindly for the phone. Dirty sock dirty underwear dirty dish, not even sure what that is… He finally found it and lifted it to his ear.

"Someone better be dead," he rasped menacingly into the phone.

"Yeah, it's about to be you, if you keep up that tone with me," his sister Malika snapped back.

Jamar grabbed his head and groaned at both the sound of her voice and… well, the sound of her voice. Malika was a beautiful woman, no doubt about that–after all, she was his sister so she got her share of the good genes - but she had a demeanor that would make a drill sergeant envious, and a voice to match. If she started that militant revolutionary shit right now, he hoped he couldn't be held responsible in a court of law for his response.

"Malika, can you call me back at a reasonable

time. Say, 2 pm... next Tuesday?" His voice, already crackled, was further muffled by the pillow he pushed over his face to block out the sunlight.

"What? I can't understand a damn thing you're saying," Malika spit into the phone. "It's not my fault you keep your ass out all night long drinking with those loser friends of yours at that dive bar! I know Black folks everywhere are celebrating Obama's election and all–which you know is really just a neoliberal plot to diffuse the power of the oppressed masses, by giving us a figurehead when our people are suffering in the street every day! But shit, get up, cause the world as we know it is about to change!" Her voice sparkled with fervor. "You're going to miss everything! Your lazy ass will thank me for this later."

Jamar licked his lips, so dry they were painful, like a dress two sizes too small. She was right about one thing at least; shoulda drank more water and less whiskey last night. But then, that wasn't a new story for him – the only difference was, for once, he had all the Black folks in Harlem, most of the Puerto Ricans and half the liberal white folks with him. Jamar didn't really care about politics. In fact, he had been too ashamed to say he hadn't voted for Obama. Shit, he hadn't voted for anybody since junior high school president... and then he'd voted for himself. But seeing Old Man Joe, a permanent fixture at Remy's Bar, crying like a baby as he talked about his father who had been lynched dreaming that such a day would come, Jamar was proud to raise up a toast. Or six.

But of course, that meant he was in a very familiar position, along with 85 percent of the nation's Black population – hung over, pissed off and losing any shreds of patience he had left. "What am I gonna miss? A good day's rest? Too late, I already missed it."

"What?" Her voice hit an octave designed to make his head crack open like a walnut shell. "You mean you really have been in bed all this time? You haven't even got up to do anything at all? Brush your teeth? Nothing? Jamar, just cause you ain't got a job, again, doesn't mean you need to be the saddest person on this planet. I'm not telling you to go work for some capitalist white supremacist oppressor, but there are so many community programs and centers that could use a brotha

IN FACT, HE HAD BEEN TOO ASHAMED TO SAY HE HADN'T VOTED FOR OBAMA. SHIT, HE HADN'T VOTED FOR ANYBODY SINCE JUNIOR HIGH SCHOOL PRESIDENT...AND THEN HE'D VOTED FOR HIMSELF.

like you. Don't buy into this post racial madness sweeping the nation – you know Obama in the White House ain't fitting to change the material conditions of the brothas and sistas on the streets! You should be involved in our community! You could be helping young cats stay out of the gang."

"At the very least you could get up and wash ya ass once in a while, damn!" Malika sighed a heavy sigh, laden with the burden of being born the younger sister to such a shiftless counterrevolutionary fool.

Jamar rubbed the short dreadlocks springing out from his head in all directions and rolled his eyes. He really did not need this shit, not so early in the afternoon... okay then, not so early in the evening. Sure, he had lost his job a week ago. And sure, it had been the ninth job this year. Yes, he had drunk up the last of his money last night, and slept so long today he hadn't had a chance to get out to look for work, like he had planned. Like he had planned every day this week. But damn, that's why he needed to drink – cause he was broke and jobless.

And her old "power to the people" routine was just too tired. Their parents had been part of the Philly chapter of the Black Panthers. They had both done time, gotten their asses beat by cops, to make a better world for their kids. Had given both Jamar and Malika African names, celebrated Kwanzaa and all that super Black shit. But this wasn't 1968 anymore. America had just proved that last night, hadn't it? This was a new day, one where Black people could truly do anything, even become president.

Power to the people, my ass. The only power Jamar was worried about right now was his electricity, since he hadn't paid the bill in about two months.

Satisfied that Jamar was properly chastised, Malika continued, "Well, if you HAD been awake at a decent hour you would have heard about the most incredible shit I ever imagined. This is a dawning of a new day for oppressed peoples around the world, big brother! And I ain't talking bout that Black puppet in the White House! Who would have thought when the revolution happened, it would come not from the third world but from another world!" She giggled uncontrollably, and for a minute, Jamar remembered the ashy-kneed little girl in braids who used to squeal when he pushed her on the rusty swing set in the school yard, demanding to be pushed higher and higher.

But of course, she had to ruin that moment. "Look, are you ready for this stuff? You sitting down? Well, knowing you, you're probably still laying down. I at least hope you have some drawers on, cause you know I hate talking to you when you naked..."

"Will you just tell me what the fuck is going on or leave me the hell alone??!" Jamar's frustrated yell felt like a hammer to his head, but he just couldn't take it anymore.

"Muthafucking aliens, muthafucka! Okay?!"

She threw the words out like daggers. "There are muthafucking aliens, they just arrived this morning, and in exactly two minutes, they are fitting to address us."

Jamar was silent for a minute. Then he said, rage leaking out of his tone at all sides, "You woke me up when I have a pounding headache to play some stupid ass game with me. So help me, Malika..."

"It's true," Malika yelled back. "These aliens from outer space are here and they want to talk! And just wait to you hear whose voice they talking with!"

The silence was deafening.

"Damnit, turn on the tv - it's all they're talking about and watch it for your damn self. That is," she retorted, "if that busted ass set of yours can even pick up a decent picture. Don't know why I even bother with you. I swear... Malcolm X, give me strength," was her parting goodbye as she hung up the phone.

"She thinks she's so funny," he muttered to himself as he tossed the phone back into the dead sea that was his bedroom floor, from whence it came.

I'm not turning on the tv, he said to himself firmly, I'm not playing along with whatever game she's up to.

Jamar closed his eyes and rolled over.

And over.

And over.

"Ah what the hell," he said, throwing off the blanket (no sheets), "I'm up, I might as well see what's on."

He threw some sweatpants over the boxers Malika would be so glad to know he was wearing, padded into the living room, and dropped down onto the couch. He dug the remote out of the crevice of the couch, along with a pizza crust, a peppermint candy still in its wrapper, and a lint ball the size of a baby's head.

He clicked the worn power button.

His pout quickly changed to a look of disbelief and amazement. His jaw dropped.

A giant chrome spaceship hovering over the capitol filled the screen on every station he flipped to. It was fairly flat and had a number of prongs that stretched out from the base. Jamar realized ruefully that it sort of looked like a space age afro pick. No wonder Malika was so excited.

The audio running with the image was of the aliens, who had used the voice pattern of revolutionary poet Gil Scott Heron. Everything they said sounded like it should have been set to the beat of a congo drum, performed in front of audiences that would snap at the completion and then go burn down some white-owned stores.

"We reach out in solidarity to the scarred peoples of the planet Earth. We do not come in peace, but in justice."

"We have traveled many light years to engage your populations in a revolutionary exchange. We have technology that can cure many diseases, that can create sustainable food growth, for soil purification, for renewable sources of energy. We have resources and knowledge to bring power to your scarred communities and enable you to establish autonomous spaces that you administer and defend. The power to determine the destinies of your own communities."

> ## WE REACH OUT IN SOLIDARITY TO THE SCARRED PEOPLES OF THE PLANET EARTH. WE DO NOT COME IN PEACE, BUT IN JUSTICE.

Autonomous spaces? Damn, Jamar said, they must have been reading those big ass dull books Malika was always trying to push on him.

"We want to be clear: we cannot just give these to you. It is not that we do not wish it. But our technology is not like yours. We do not build something independent of ourselves. To create something new, we, all of us, must grow it together, each putting in pieces of ourselves. By giving, we are all enriched."

Jamar snorted. Sounds like a pyramid scam. If they threw in a trip to Hawaii, they'd get more suckers to bite.

"But we can commit to staying here and working with you until these technologies are fully birthed."

"Please understand, though, this is not charity, but an act of solidarity."

If this was a Gil Scott poem, this is where everyone would have snapped.

"Because we must devote individuals, equipment and resources, we can only focus on a part of your planet at a time. So right now, our offer is only open to those scarred peoples in the country called the United States of America."

Scarred peoples? Jamar thought. Is that what this cat keeps saying? Did he mean scared and it was just a glitch in the translation?

"In exchange for this, we ask that the scarred people of the United States of America commit to joining us in liberating other scarred peoples in the galaxy for the next eight of your earth years, and help us create autonomous communities open to all scarred people everywhere. This is how we are able to bring this to your planet, and we believe it only right to continue to pass along the aid we receive."

"Scarred people of the United States, we picked you because we monitored your recent history. We saw all scarred communities coming together to protest unjust wars, challenge abuses of power, and work to create a new world.

We saw your young take to the streets in rage and hope. We heard the voices of your greatest philosophers, like the one whose voice I now use to speak to you, and it resonated deeply in us as we too know that the revolution will not be televised, not be televised, the revolution will be no rerun brothas (and sistas) the revolution will be live."

Jamar started. They were talking about the 1960s – but that was so long ago. Either they got their wires crossed and messed up on the time, or time passes real different for them than for us humans, us scarred people, whatever that is. Malika must be shitting herself with joy.

"Scarred people of the United States, you have a week to decide."

"Dig it."

The end of the transmission created a typhoon of commentary on television and radio stations: What did an 'autonomous community' mean? What would they be liberating? And what the hell were scarred people?

Gil Scott's rich voice cut back in, silencing the cacophony. "We understand. 'Scarred peoples' is the term we have created to represent all of us who have experienced the exploitation of our labor, our culture, our histories and our bodies by populations promulgated upon a fraudulent hierarchical genetic supposition based on visual demarcations of difference."

The silence was deafening.

"Look," Gil said starting to sound a little irked, "We come from many planets, many races and species. We have joined together because we have been oppressed on our homeworlds. I am from the first scarred peoples to rise up. We freed ourselves, with the solidarity of scarred peoples from a nearby star. We made the commitment to do the same for others, and to grow our ranks of scarred liberators. We are here, speaking to the scarred peoples of the Unites States of America. Those who have suffered from this brutality so familiar to our own, what you call white supremacy, racism, colonization."

"We are speaking only to those who have decided to call yourselves 'people of color.' Can you dig it now?" Gil must not have been as confident in our power of collective comprehension because he added, "So those of yall who ain't white."

"We await your reply."

The airwaves exploded. Phone lines jammed as people across the country called into talk radio. On Fox News, commentators foamed at the mouth, each screaming over each other. "This is reverse discrimination!" "We should take this as a direct attack against our way of life!" "These aliens are jealous of normal Americans' freedoms!" "The U.S. military knows more about bringing freedom to places than anywhere else on the globe: just look at Iraq and Afghanistan – just ask Vietnam! Maybe we should show these aliens a little of how we bring liberation, American style!"

The calls for military action were, however, somewhat muted after a display of power by the alien spaceship which, with one burst of its lasers, disabled every weapon in the entire Washington D.C. area, down to every warhead, missile, bomb and handgun.

What about Obama? People, especially

WE KNOW, FROM CENTURIES OF EXPERIENCE WORKING IN INTERGALACTIC SOLIDARITY, THAT THIS WILL NOT CHANGE YOUR SITUATION FOR THE BETTER, AND PERHAPS IT WILL MAKE IT MUCH WORSE.

white people, especially *especially* white liberals, implored. *We just elected the first Black president in the history of the country yesterday. Doesn't that count for anything?*

"Not really," Gil was definitely more than a little peeved at the unexpected slowness. Guess he was planning on landing in the middle of a Black Panther rally, Jamar thought. "On our planet we had some of our kind who were in positions of power. That in no way changed the conditions of the masses of scarred people who were enslaved and exploited. We know, from centuries of experience working in intergalactic solidarity, that this will not change your situation for the better, and perhaps it will make it much worse. We have seen that after a token advancement such as this, the backlash against the scarred peoples is indescribable, often setting back the cause for liberation decades."

"But, as it should be, as it ever was, the choice is yours, scarred peoples of USA."

Jamar leaned back on his ratty couch, absentmindedly unwrapped the peppermint candy and popped it in his mouth, which was still hanging open. "Well, the shit's bout to hit the fan now, isn't it?" Jamar asked the empty room in wonder. **ⓑ**

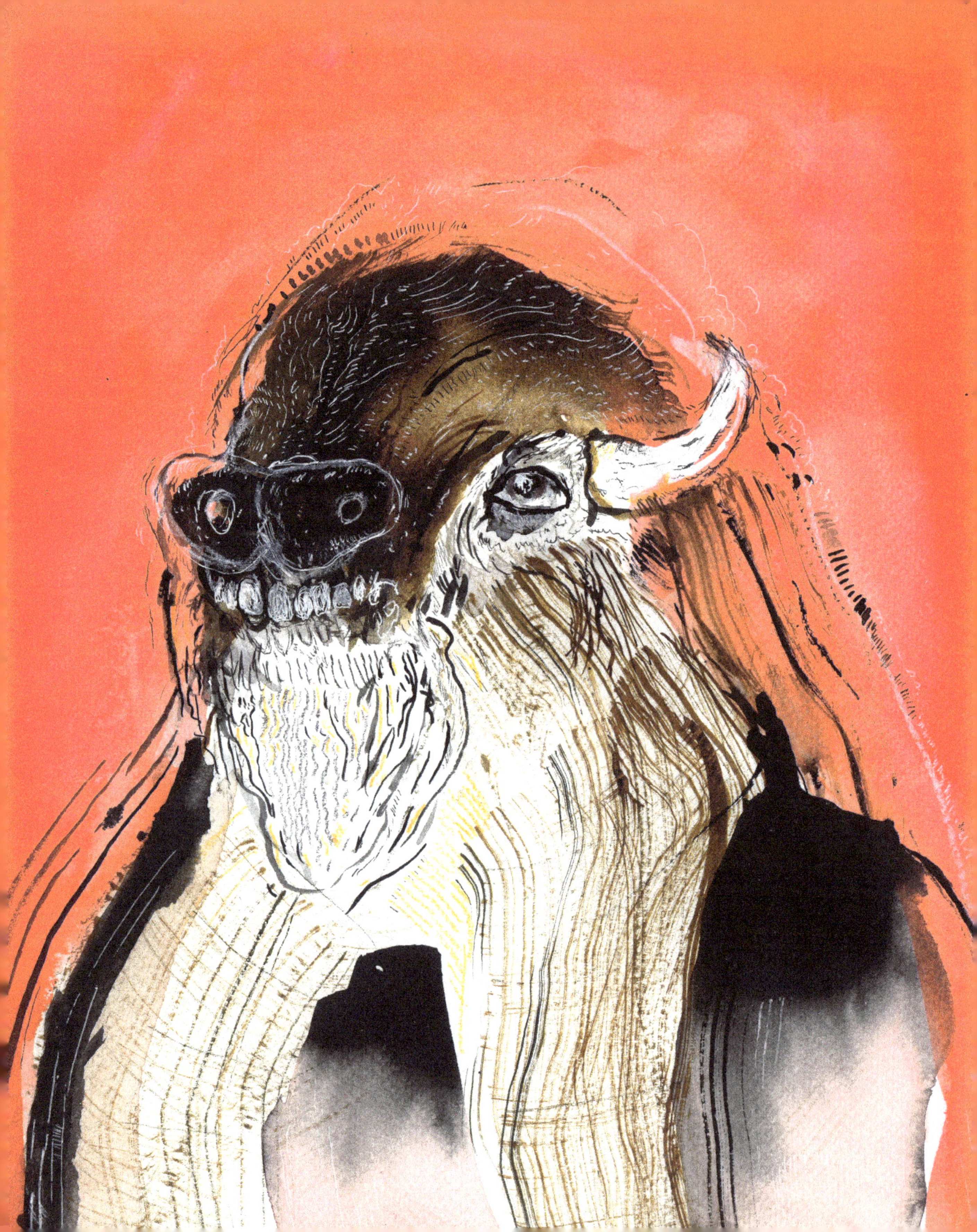

WILD BUFFALOES

Words by Justin Hocking
Artwork by Sean Croghan

Justin Hocking is the author of *The Great Floodgates of the Wonderworld: A Memoir,* winner of the Oregon Book Award and a finalist for the PEN Center USA Prize for Creative Nonfiction. His fiction and nonfiction have also appeared in *The Normal School, Orion, Poets & Writers* Magazine, *The Portland Mercury* and elsewhere. "Wild Buffaloes" is excerpted from a short fiction collection-in-progress, and his first poetry chapbook, entitled PS: *The Wolves,* will be released by Two Plum Press in October 2019. He teaches writing at Portland State University.

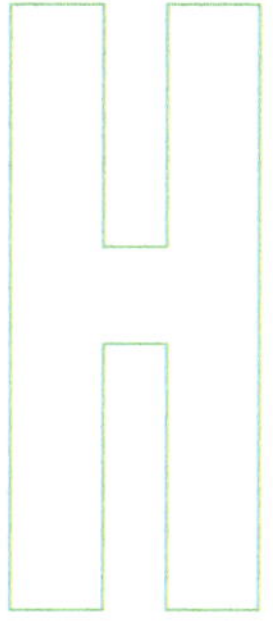

How would you describe yourself?

I think the words in English are "brick shithouse."

Meaning you're big?

My mother used to say I'm like a buffalo. Anyone think they can knock me down? I dare you. Only one man has ever knocked me down in my life. That man was driving a car.

Where did that happen?

El Salvador.

That's where you're from?

Yes, the city of San Salvador.

How long have you been in the States?

Maybe fifteen months now. A long time.

What do you do here?

I build houses. Sometimes fences. Or dig up stumps.

What about back in El Salvador?

I was a teacher. Martial arts. I taught people not to fear. I welcomed everyone to my studio. I wanted to make everyone feel strong.

What happened? Why did you leave?

It started when a gay person came to my studio and I taught him what he needed to know. Then he told his friends, and they told their friends, and pretty soon I taught all the people. They needed to protect themselves, especially in El Salvador, and I helped them.

And then?

Some bad people in our town found out what I was doing. They came in and told me not to teach any more gay people.

What'd you say?

I told them to go fuck yourself! I said any one of you want to fight, let's go! All these tough gangsters with tattooed faces, but no one would take me on. That was my turf. They were afraid.

I went home that night and told my mother what happened. She said I better get out of town, that I was in *mucho peligro*.

I went to my studio the next day. All the windows were broken, and they threw a dead animal inside.

What kind of animal?

Hard to say. Too much blood.

What did you do?

I cleaned up. Covered all the windows with wood. Finished just in time to teach my classes that day. Some of my people came and saw what happened, and they were scared. They didn't want to come to class. But I said now more than ever you need to protect yourself.

So they stayed?

They stayed. They took class. We trained hard that day.

And then?

We kept going like that for one week, two weeks.

Were you scared?

Do I look like a scared person?

I was scared for my people, though, so I trained them harder and harder.

But then one day, driving home, two cars pulled up on either side of my jeep. They shot out all the windows with handguns.

Jesus. Did you get hit?

No. They were just trying to scare me again.

But you don't get scared . . .

No man. You know who gets scared? My mother. She put me on a plane two days later. She said ██████ you have to get out of here or you'll end up dead, my only son. So now here I am.

You feel safe here?

Sure, until I get sent back.

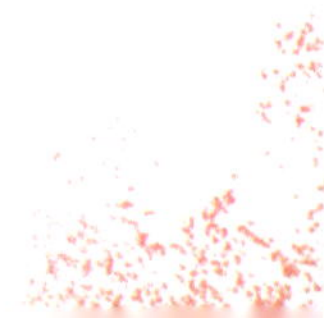

You think they'll still remember you, the gangsters?
Si, claro! (laughs).

But you've been gone over a year. And you're not teaching anymore.
The story's not over. About two months ago. A friend from El Salvador calls me, says one of the gangsters who threatened me was here in Portland.

Oh shit.
Yeah oh shit.

So then?
I borrowed a gun from a guy I know. I went to the house where the man was. I waited in the bushes for a long time. Just sitting there for one hour, two hour, three hours. It got dark and I still waited. Then the man finally came out. I ran for him. Knocked him down in the grass and aimed the gun.

He begged me not to shoot. He said over and over, ██████, please don't shoot me. He was crying. I held him like that with the gun for a long time.

But you didn't . . .
No, I don't want to kill no one.

You let him go?
He pissed in his pants he was so scared. Then I let him go.

Did you feel better after?
(. . .)

Maybe that wasn't the right question.
I felt ok, until later when my mother called.

She knew what happened?
No. But I realized it's a long time until I see her again.

Right. When will that be?
Maybe in a year I'll make enough to bring her here.

What if you get deported? Will you see her then?
If I get deported I'm dead.

Would you describe yourself as a refugee?
I describe myself as a buffalo! I'm just going to roam around for a while. That's what buffaloes do, right? ⏸

(With thanks to *W.*)

MISSED CONNECTIONS #2:
POST TRAUMATIC LATTE?

Excerpts from the novel in progress,
The Ballad of Amber Ines Arthur

Words by Joel Preston Smith
Artwork by Brianna Spencer

Joel Preston Smith is a writer, artist and disaster responder. He's the author of *Night of a Thousand Stars & Other Portraits of Iraq*, published by Nazraeli Press (2006) and nominated for the Oregon Book Award for nonfiction in 2007. His website is joelprestonsmith.com.

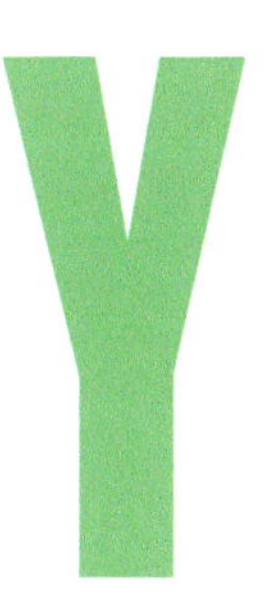

You: Super-hot with initials E.R. in black Sharpie on waistband of olive-green scrubs.

Me: Medium length wavy ginger hair, tidy goatee, tat of black heraldic eagle superior to left tricep, transverse fracture of the inferior nasal concha, transverse fracture of right humerus proximal to lesser tubercle, comminuted fracture of left trapezium, art-college faculty identification card with lanyard in attitude of vasoconstriction vis-a-vis right common carotid artery/right external jugular vein/dorsal veinous arch of foot (the left one), and competition-grade target arrow dorso-lateral to, and protrudent from, left lung.

Ringing in ears. Bleeding from same. Occipital hematoma. Parietal contusion. Patellar

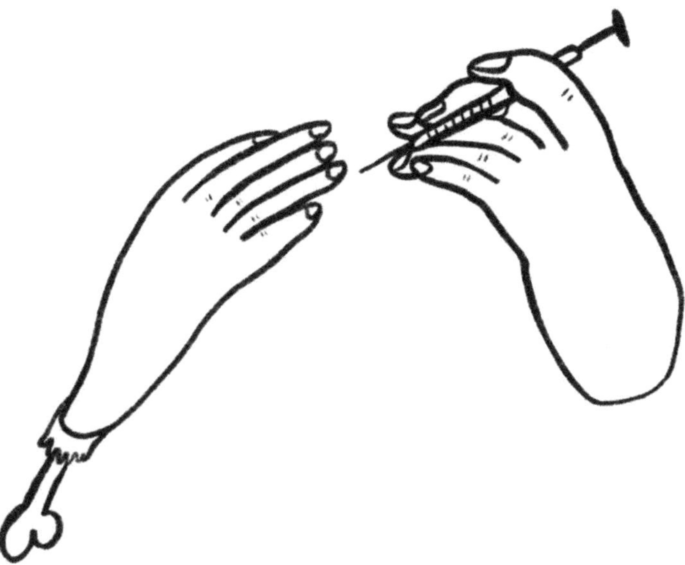

and scapular subcutaneous bruising, etc. They'd just carried me from the helicopter. You patted my hand, the serpentine tendrils of your flaxen ringlets spilling like golden fountains from the elastic band of your disposable surgical cap.

You asked me if it hurt. I said, softly, "Very, very much."

I did not happen to catch your name. Erin? Eva? Ella? Emma? Elisha? Eliza? Emilia? Esmerelda? Etta? Effie? Essie? Is it forward of me to ask the given surname of the thoughtful, considerate woman to whom I owe my life? May I buy you a cup of hot coffee? Unless that's some kind of Hippocratic ethics infraction.

Romero? Rabinovitz?

I hate the idea of thinking about you doing chest compressions and screaming for another 80cc's of adrenalin and then, when I finally get to meet you in person, fully conscious and coherent, going Dutch. I'm sure you're terribly busy. I could meet you somewhere convenient. Canteen? Starbucks? There's one two blocks north of the Intensive Care Unit, kitty corner to Coffee People. Tomorrow? The next day? Wednesday?

I'm not expected back at the college until mid-October, after the stitches and the steel pins and plates come out and I've been cleared by the neurologist and the podiatrist and the pulmonologist and the occupational therapist and the head of the Division of Otolaryngology, whose name I forget (still with the migraines and the spontaneous vitreous fireworks).

It is entirely your call. Thursday? ⓑ

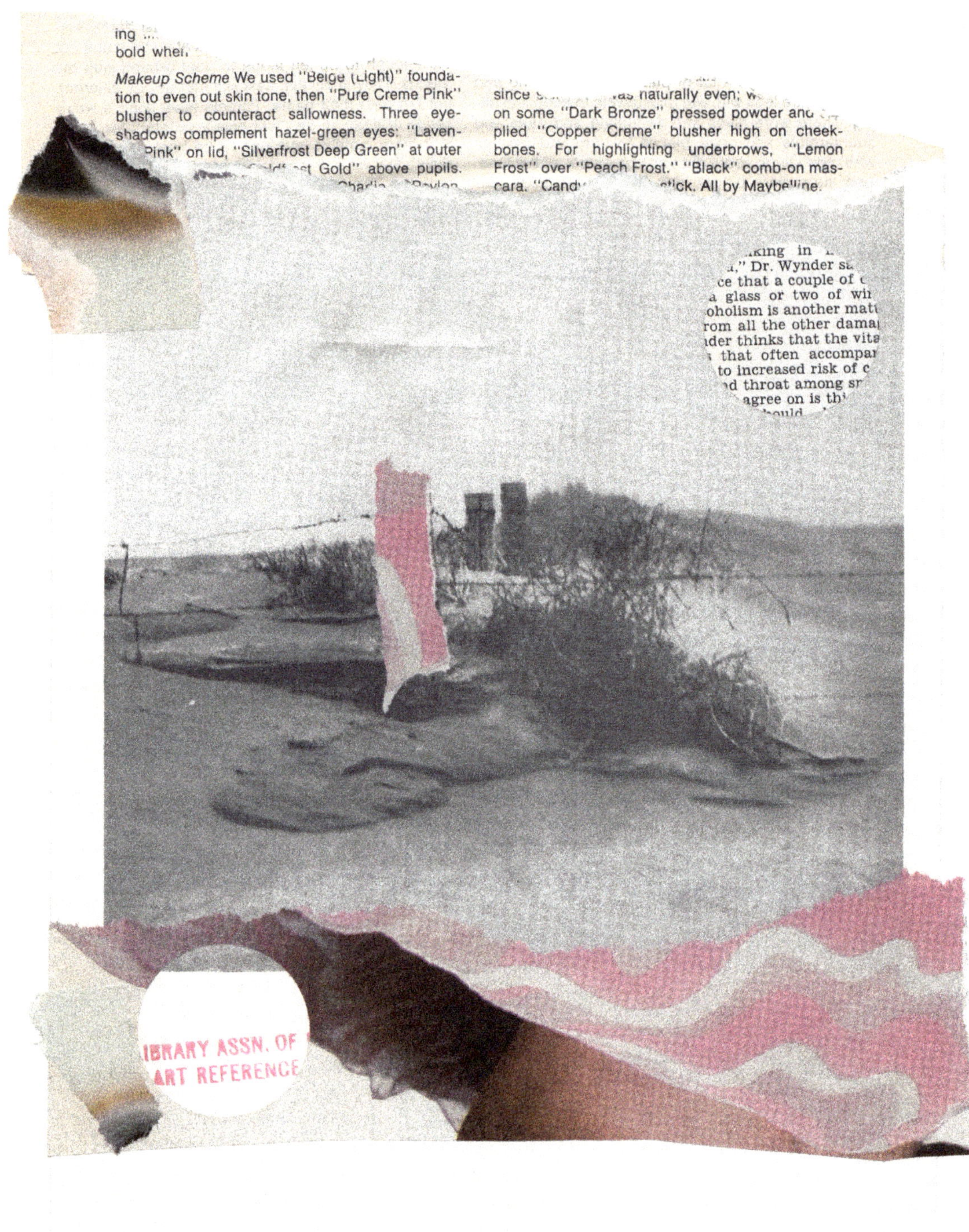

Makeup Scheme We used ''Beige (Light)'' foundation to even out skin tone, then ''Pure Creme Pink''
blusher to counteract sallowness. Three eye-
shadows complement hazel-green eyes: ''Laven-
Pink'' on lid, ''Silverfrost Deep Green'' at outer
Gold'' above pupils.
since s was naturally even; w
on some ''Dark Bronze'' pressed powder and
plied ''Copper Creme'' blusher high on cheek-
bones. For highlighting underbrows, ''Lemon
Frost'' over ''Peach Frost.'' ''Black'' comb-on mascara. ''Cand stick. All by Maybelline.
king in
,'' Dr. Wynder s
ce that a couple of
a glass or two of wi
oholism is another matt
rom all the other dama
der thinks that the vita
that often accompan
to increased risk of c
d throat among sr
agree on is th

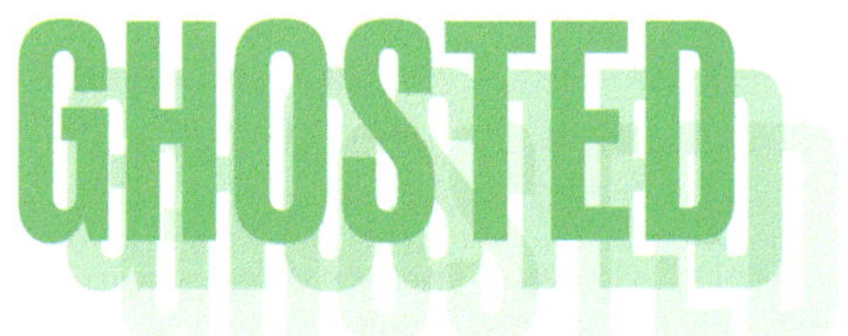

GHOSTED

Words by Susan DeFreitas
Artwork by Shannon O'Connor

Susan DeFreitas has never been able to choose between fantasy and reality, so she lives and writes in both. A first-generation American of Caribbean descent, she is the author of the novel *Hot Season*, which won a Gold IPPY Award for Best Fiction of the Mountain West; her fiction, nonfiction and poetry has been featured in the *Writer's Chronicle*, the *Huffington Post*, the *Utne Reader*, *Story Magazine*, *Daily Science Fiction*, *High Desert Journal*, and many other journals and anthologies. In 2017, *The Oregonian* named her "One of 25 Oregon Authors Every Oregonian Must Read."

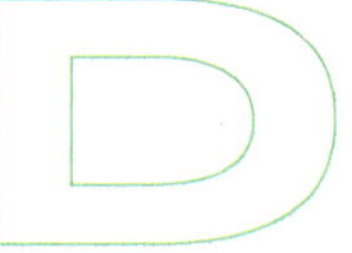ating anywhere is difficult, but dating in a city full of seasonally affected passive-aggressive depressives like yourself is worse, especially when it is the end of October in the soggy Northwest and the long gloom of winter looms and you are thirty-two and recently, unexpectedly single and are more comfortable, generally speaking, in a bookstore than you are in a bar.

I spent my days off in the quiet aisles of Powell's, in the Blue Room and the Gold, amid the whispered hush of conversations—in the bookstore's café, where the origami savant sat, day after day, rocking to the rhythm of his own personal train, perpetually folding paper, where bespectacled teenagers hunched companionably over manga.

After the breakup, I sought out a certain book there, one I had loved in grad school, an epistolary mystery. I had given away my only copy—or perhaps lost it in the split—and now, considering how much more expensive it was to live alone, I didn't feel like I could purchase it again just yet. There I stood in the A-B aisle, rereading one of my favorite passages—the one in which the lovers in the modern timeline of the novel admit their shared obsession with the lovers in the past—when a note fell out on the floor.

Folded stationary with a scalloped edge—my heart quickened at the paper, creamy smooth with fine grains of wood pulp visible within it. The handwriting was a series of slanted lines, written in a fine-point pen.

This is my favorite book of all time. Is it yours too? If so, you may be the one for me, and me the one for you.

Why not? Dating in this town sucks!

They say love is never wondering—though honestly, I'm not so sure.

Yours (perhaps?),

X

Someone had given this book as a gift at some point and included this note between its pages. It was an obvious conclusion, supported by an obvious fact: Powell's sold both new and used books. And yet the copy I held appeared to be the former, its spine intact, uncracked.

That was how it began, in those dark first weeks, post Paul. Dark literally, north of the 45th parallel, and figuratively as well, considering the fact that I, in some desperate suspension of disbelief—as if I myself were the protagonist of a novel—slid that note into my purse, pulled out a postcard I found there and actually composed a reply to X, this mystery person, who may have been no more than the former love interest of the former owner of this book. I folded my response between the pages of the novel, slid it back onto the shelf, and returned to bookstore's café, where I gathered up my ratty wool coat and left, stepping into the damp gray gloom outside.

In my pocket was the small stone I'd found there, after I'd purchased the coat from Goodwill—a roundish gray one. I'd always imagined the former owner of this coat had picked this stone up somewhere on the Oregon Coast, in the course of a long walk with her lover. But lately I imagined that she'd come upon it by herself, thinking the sort of thoughts a woman thinks by herself, watching the sun set out over the ocean. There was nothing remarkable about the stone, as far as I could tell; the former owner of this coat must have picked it up to remind her of something. Something I would never know.

Nevertheless, I cradled that stone as I walked down Burnside to catch the 72, turning it over gently in my hand, as if it were something

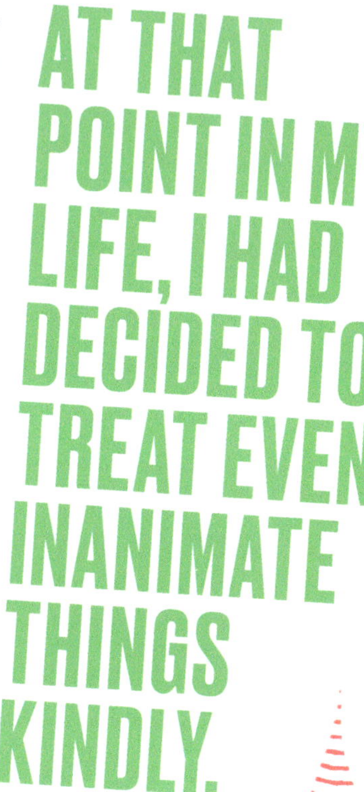

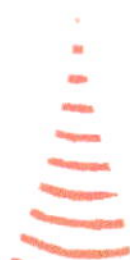

precious to me. At that point in my life, I had decided to treat even inanimate things kindly.

Looking back now, I could see that Paul had never really been there for me. Maybe never really been there for himself. Despite his conspicuous coloration, that bright-red shock of hair I'd found so endearing, Paul seemed to move through the world like a ghost, never really touching things, never truly seeing them. I would not live that way. I would allow myself a sense of tenderness toward the world at large, even if it hurt.

In my response to X, I'd written:

I'm not sure this book is my favorite, but it's up there, for sure. As far as dating goes, I think people in this town only fall in love when they're trying not to. Anyway, that's how it happened for me, last time around.

A word to the wise: Don't go on a second date with anyone who was late to the first. (And if you meet a ginger named Paul who's a big fan of The Clash, tell him I want my *Saga* omnibus back.)

Yours (possibly),

Y

When I returned to Powell's a week later and checked the book, my postcard was gone, replaced by another fine fold of stationary, another note written with that fine-point pen. It was perhaps the finest fine point I had ever seen.

My dear Y,

I will do my best not to fall in love with you if you do the same for me. Who wants to fall, anyway? I'd rather stand at the top and enjoy the view.

Metaphorically speaking—all I see when I stand here in this aisle is this book, which I love, and others I do not yet know enough to. Maybe that's enough. To know you've stood here, will stand here too, surrounded by all these stories, most of them—and maybe all the good ones—too good to be true.

What strange creatures we are, that we can feel so much for imaginary people, those who once lived and wrote and now are dead, and those wholly imagined characters, those who never lived at all.

Are you? Imaginary too?

Yours,

X

Windlessness. An afterimage. The sensation of standing on a ship at sea later that day, at dock. The sensation of a thing caused by the absence of that thing: that's what I felt the day X replied.

Him? Her? They? Zir? I had no idea what this person's pronouns might be. Frankly did not care. Even if I was being played, there was nothing casual about this game; the quality of the stationary, of the pen, the penmanship (*now there's a gendered term*, I thought), betrayed the care with which this flirtation had been entered into.

We wrote back and forth this way over the holidays, until the glittering trappings of New Year's were soggy trash on the city's sidewalks. I told X about Paul, the way he'd dumped me by disappearing into the aisles of Home Depot, informing me later via text. ("I just don't see us building this bookshelf together.") Leaving me no choice but to MAX it back from fucking Beaverton. The way Paul had dumped my stuff (most of it, anyway) at Mara's, changed the locks, and totally ghosted on me—after two years together, the man had not responded to a single communication on my part. ("Unconscionable," X pronounced it.) I told X about the manuscript I was working on, between bouts of crying and data entry. ("Kind of like *Fear of Flying*, but without the sex and psychoanalysis.")

X told me about their ex, whom they claimed to have lost to the circus. ("But who among us has not heard the siren song of aerial dance, the swaying silken *tissu*?") About the books that had gotten them through the breakup. ("Bigger is better," they wrote. "And Liz Gilbert is apparently somewhat questionable as a person, but *The Signature of All Things* is beyond question.") About their dog, Herbert, a weinerhuahua who could not help but wet himself in excitement every time the doorbell rang.

Sometimes a new note appeared every day, but sometimes I was forced to wait an entire week,

returning each morning to find my own note still tucked between the pages of *Possession*. It was that book, I realized, that had sparked my fondest conceptions of romantic love. Why hadn't I read any others by the same author?

One by one, I checked them out of the library, and one by one I read them, even the doorstopper with the trim size of a tablet computer. By the time I finished it, I felt as if as if I'd lived the lives of ten different people, all of whom had lived through a war.

I also checked out the first *Saga* omnibus, then the second—once upon a time, I had imagined myself as Alana and Paul as Marko, two renegade revolutionaries on the run (from

what, at this point, seemed hard to say). Now I imagined X as Marko—literally, with the ram's horns, chiseled jaw, and all. I had no idea what this person actually looked like, so why not?

Hanging out before work in the bookstore's café, I plucked books from the reshelf cart at random, which is how I wound up reading Jaron Lanier's *Seven Arguments for Deleting Your Social Media Accounts Right Now*. Instead of deleting my social media accounts, I considered the science of addiction. Apparently, it wasn't just the promise of a new message or alert that kept us perpetually glued to our phones, it was the peril of finding nothing, the threat of disappointment, which made interacting on social media a lot like gambling. I thought I might know something about that kind of addiction, returning to lthe A–B aisle for the seventh time in two hours—not that I was keeping track. The rush of discovering a new note, the three-inch drop of not.

Did I try to solve for X, so to speak? Constantly, at first. Hanging out by the help desk, surreptitiously checking out anyone who slipped into the A–B. Standing at Customer Look Up, glancing over my shoulder so often, I imagined, the booksellers must have wondered if I was being stalked. Of course, I was the stalker—sort of. But no matter how faithfully I monitored the aisle, I never saw anyone pick up that copy of *Possession*.

Was X an employee? If so, the pace at which new notes appeared never fit any pattern, any regular rotation of shifts. I could not even tell whether the notes arrived during the day or the night, morning or afternoon—only that sometimes one would appear while I was still in the bookstore, which was maddening. I never caught so much as a glimpse of X.

Of course, that did not prevent me from developing a list of possible candidates—the loping, sloppily handsome bookseller with the English accent, for example, and the thin, intense goth girl of indeterminate age. In the course of a month, I developed and discarded a half dozen such fixations, all the while knowing that X might just as likely be the origami artist, one of the manga teens, or the bosomy bookseller in the peasant skirt.

Though I never saw X, I assumed that they saw me, so I dressed for my trips to the bookstore. Perhaps even consciously cultivating some sexy librarian sort of androgyny. I didn't know X's gender—best, I thought, to play it safe. I shaved my head in the back and on the sides, dyed what was left a mossy green. I didn't have the wings, of course, but I figured maybe X would get it: I looked just a bit like Alana from *Saga*. There seemed to be no literary reference too obscure for this person, whether high-brow or low, no geekery beyond the pale. Unlike Paul, who'd always claimed comics were for kids. Why had I even tried with that guy? Why, at the price of my *Saga* omnibus, which had cost me a whopping sixty bucks, purchased at a time in my life when I'd considered cream cheese a luxury?

I might still have been strapped, but I wasn't in grad school anymore. I'd gone full time at work, cutting back on the hours set aside for my novel—since Paul had left me, I hadn't been working on it anyway. I figured I'd return to it at some point; in the meantime, I was happy to be able to pay my bills, to cover little extravagances like sulfate-free shampoo, and to shop a better grade of secondhand than I'd previously been able to afford.

When I tried on clothes in The Buffalo Exchange I imagined what X might say, sitting on a chair outside the changing room. *My dear,* they'd say, *I will do my best not to fall in love with you, but in that dress?*

I imagined Marko's chiseled chin in X's hand. The slow smile when I walked their way. Shaking those heavy horns. Day by day, despite the fact that I was no longer writing, I was living in fiction, much of it of my own making.

All that reading. All that preening. All that imagining myself through my ghost lover's eyes. Was I falling for X, or was I falling for Y?

I noticed people watching me. Men, women, boys, girls, and those of mixed genders too. They started conversations—about the book I was reading on the train, about the excellent vegan whiskey bar on Belmont, about the difficulty of discouraging moss from taking up residence on your roof. It took me forever to realize these people were hitting on me.

I smiled, made conversation. But I never called the numbers these people gave me, never went to their art openings or accepted their invites to connect on social media. Somehow, it felt as if doing so would be untrue to X.

ALL THAT READING. ALL THAT PREENING. ALL THAT IMAGINING MYSELF THROUGH MY GHOST LOVER'S EYES. WAS I FALLING FOR X, OR WAS I FALLING FOR Y?

"So, who is he?" my friend Mara asked. We were sitting in the vegan whiskey bar, which was indeed excellent, eating Frito pie.

"Who is who?"

"This guy. Obviously, you're seeing someone."

I arched my brows. Obviously? This guy?

"The queer hair? The pencil skirts? Penny loafers and push-up bras? Yes," she went on, before I could object, "I can tell."

I shrugged. The fact was, I wasn't seeing X at all, despite all best efforts to the contrary. "It's just a flirtation."

"With who?" Mara had been my friend since before Paul, whom she'd always dissed as a douche. (*Mental note: Pay attention to Mara.*)

"I'm not sure," I admitted.

Mara frowned. "You're not sure who you're flirting with? Like, what? This is just online?"

"Yeah," I said, "sort of."

She narrowed her eyes. "You're being very mysterious."

"It's just kind of hard to—"

"Do you think you're being catfished? Like, has this guy misrepresented himself?"

"I'm not sure it's a guy." I sipped my Pendleton Rye. "Really, they haven't represented themselves at all."

"As in, you have no idea at all what the story is with this person?"

I shrugged. "I know a bit about their ex, and their dog. Mostly, with us, it's about books."

Mara set aside my whiskey sour. Took my hands in her own, to either side of our Frito pie. "Ellin," she said, "I'm saying this as a friend. You can't let this go any further. You have to find out who this person is."

Nodding, nodding, nodding. I was conscious of that motion, so close to rocking—like the origami artist, to my own personal train. "All right," I said. "Okay."

I SHRUGGED. THE FACT WAS, I WASN'T SEEING X AT ALL, DESPITE ALL BEST EFFORTS TO THE CONTRARY.

I hadn't meant it at the time—just wanted to get her off my back—but later that night, I realized it was true. This had gone too far. I had to know.

Dearest X,

Words can't express what a comfort you've been to me, what a friend. This is my favorite conversation, and I never want it to end. But I can't continue this way, not knowing who you are.

My name is Ellinor Anders. My number is XXX-XXX-XXXX. I don't care what your gender is, or what you look like. Please text, or even call, if you're feeling bold—or, if you must, find me online.

Until next time,

Y

But somehow I knew, even as I enclosed my note in that book—our book, *Possession*, which neither of us possessed—there would be no next time.

When I returned to Powell's the next day, the book was gone. And gone it stayed, for nearly two weeks, though it appeared to be in stock at Customer Look Up.

Poor little human heart, which must expand to accommodate so much love. Poor, precious organ, which must find a way to carry on its good-natured work even when the rib cage is crushed. Over and over again, standing in the A–B aisle of the Blue Room, my chest contracted. And expanded again.

I returned faithfully to the bookstore each day, just as I had checked my phone, my voicemail, and my email over and over in those first few weeks, post-Paul. All the while knowing that this person who had meant so much to me, who'd seemed like such a kindred spirit, had ghosted on me, just like Paul. Perhaps it was my fate, I thought, to love people who weren't really there.

But one day, in the place of the missing book, I found another—the latest *Saga* omnibus. Inside the front cover was a gift receipt; the book had been purchased from Powell's the day before, with cash. A note was included, my last from X, on that creamy stationary, with all of its wood grains exposed, in that fine, slanting hand, which made me want to weep.

Y, my dear,

I am so very sorry. But it is, as yet, too soon for me to fall.

If I could, know that I would, for you.

Yours always,

X

Were those words true? I did not know, and I found, in time, I did not care. We'd found each other, X and Y, like stones in the pockets of a secondhand coat. We'd held each other for a while, carried each other from one place to another. Whoever this person was, they'd set me down gently, like something precious to them, and walked away. At that point in my life, I understood that as a kindness. ⓑ

Following spread: Alyson Provax, 2019

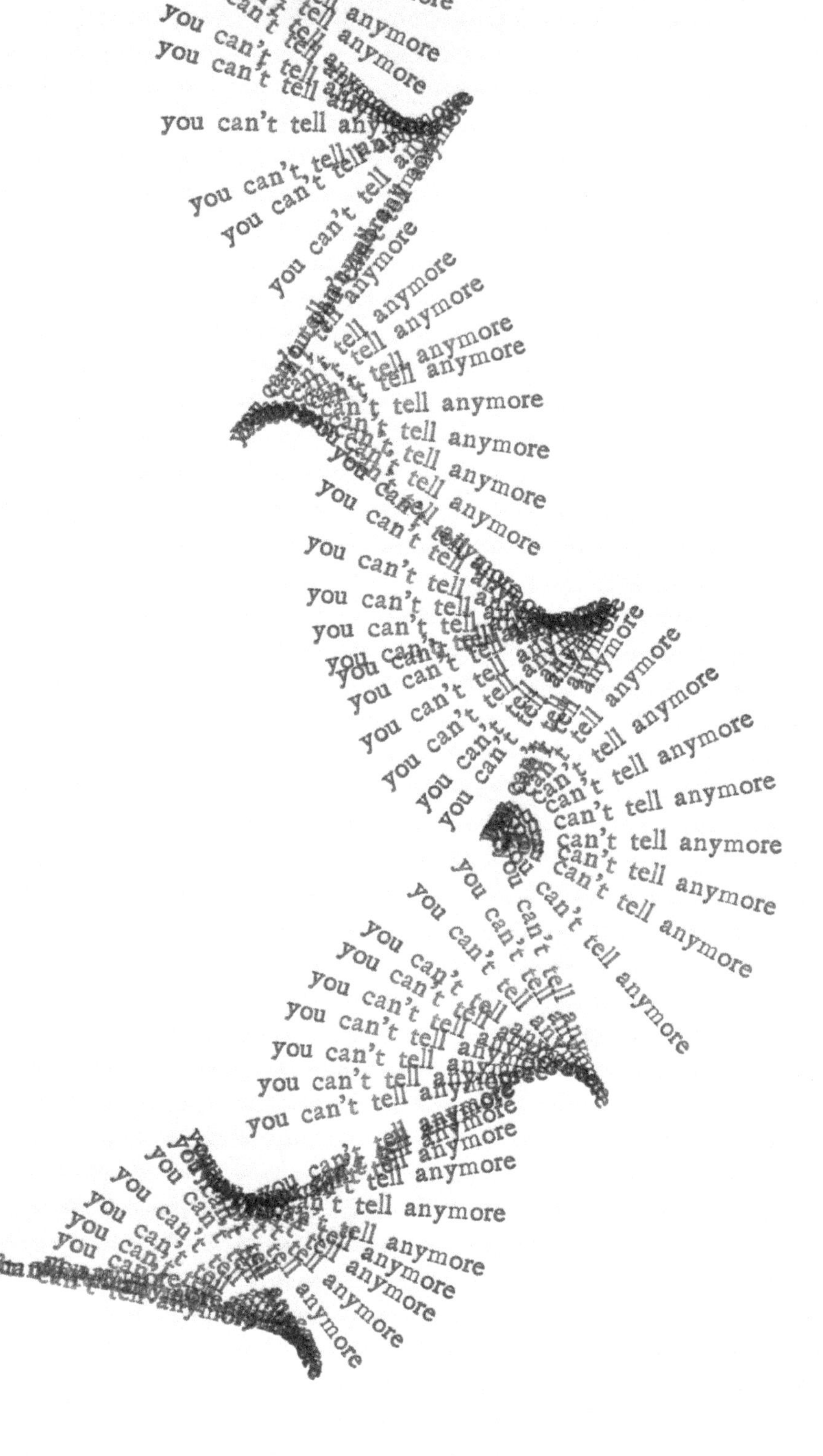

you can't tell anymore
you can't tell anymore
you can't tell anymore
you can't tell anymore
you can't tell anymore
you can't tell anymore
you can't tell anymore
tell anymore
tell anymore
tell anymore
can't tell anymore
can't tell anymore
can't tell anymore
you can't tell anymore
you can't tell anymore
you can't tell anymore
you can't tell anymore
you can't tell anymore
you can't tell anymore
you can't tell anymore
you can't tell anymore
can't tell anymore
can't tell anymore
can't tell anymore
can't tell anymore
you can't tell anymore
you can't tell anymore
you can't tell anymore
you can't tell anymore
you can't tell anymore
you can't tell anymore
you can't tell anymore
you can't tell anymore
you can't tell anymore
anymore
anymore

I felt something   but couldn't say

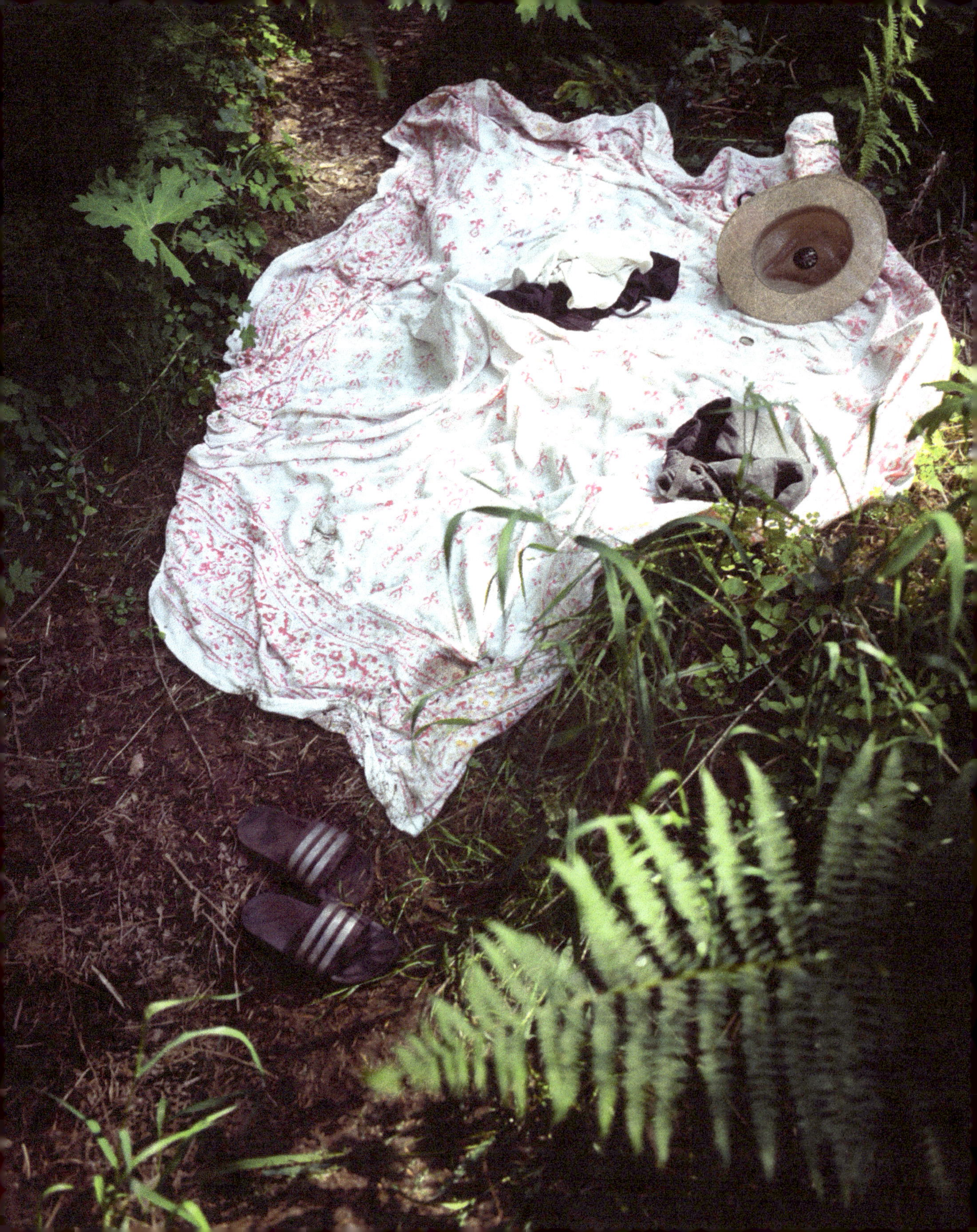

UNDERGROWTH

Words by Miranda Schmidt
Artwork by Aaron Wessling

Miranda Schmidt's work has appeared in *TriQuarterly, Orion, Catapult, Electric Literature, The Collagist,* and other journals. She has taught creative writing at the Loft, the University of Washington, and Portland Community College. Miranda grew up in the midwest and now lives in Portland. They are currently at work on a novel about haunting and a series of lyric essays that explore ecology through a queer feminist lens.

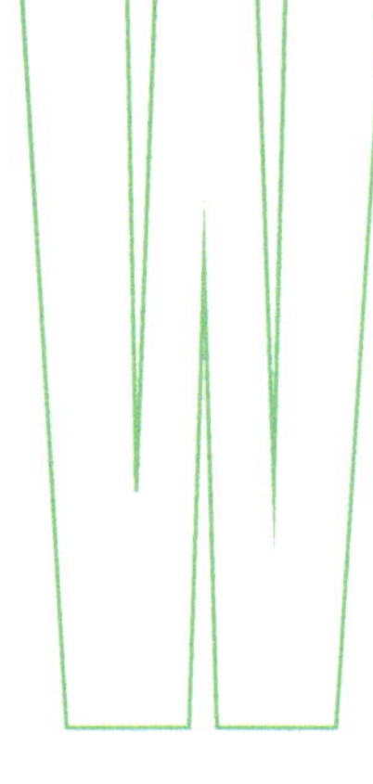

When the two people come into the woods, they bring their noise with them. They crackle old leaves in new hiking boots, snap pictures and laugh as they point at birds and flowers. But, as they move deeper into the forest, they begin to turn quiet. They begin to tread softly. They no longer touch but, instead, keep a small distance between them. They look small and bright and strange set against the dark roots and the deep green ferns. The trees watch as the couple clears out a space for themselves, as they shoo away leaves and needles and twigs, baring the dirt, before placing their tent. The trees listen when they drive their plastic spikes into the ground.

Susan and John set up their tent by the creek in the small deserted clearing, too deep in the woods, too lacking in SUV hookups and close, convenient car parking to be attractive to the families that clutter the more accessible parts of the forest. This part of the woods is pristine: no broken bottles, not one forgotten children's toy in sight.

John breathes, gathering the scents of the needles and the dirt, the leaves and water and sky, as if, Susan thinks, he could bottle them up deep in the dark of his lungs and keep them there forever.

"Perfect," he says, breathing out.

Susan tries a smile, feeling the tightness in the corners of her mouth as she glances out at the spaces between the trees that surround their campsite, spaces filled up with thick moss and saplings and shadow.

+++++

Months ago, Susan watched from the window as the old elm tree vanished: first the branches swaying outside the living room, leaves rustling in the breezes to make music with the street sounds and pictures with the sky. Then, bit by bit, they took the trunk.

Diseased trees, the notice had said when the city slipped it under the apartment door after tagging all the neighborhood trunks with yellow bands, *traffic slowed Friday through Saturday... no parking...apologies for inconvenience...*

Susan watched the cars drift by on the street below the apartment, slowing as they came through the neighborhood, as if they were trying to tread lightly with heavy tires. The drivers craned their necks to watch the men in orange vests load

for swelling. Still flat, but soon.

Soon, she whispered to herself, and wondered if a baby's kicking felt anything like branches tapping on a windowpane. She'd never gotten that far—to the kicking part. This time. Soon.

+++++

"Soon," John says when she asks him when they'll have a fire going.

He is trying to remember how to arrange the logs.

"There's a particular way," he says. "We learned it back in Boy Scouts."

He taps at his phone, scrolling through pictures and diagrams while Susan sits on a fallen tree and scratches at fallen leaves with her foot. Digging down through the dry top layer to the wet decomposition beneath, she tries to reach the solid dirt below, the hard-packed certain ground.

"Found it!" John says, holding his phone out to show her the neatly stacked kindling.

+++++

In the city, the trees were held by tight concrete circles, surrounded by sidewalks and road. But their street was bare now, leafless and shadeless, exposed. In the apartment, Susan placed a bonsai tree on the kitchen windowsill between the aloe plant and the lucky bamboo.

SUSAN WATCHED THE CARS DRIFT BY ON THE STREET BELOW THE APARTMENT, SLOWING AS THEY CAME THROUGH THE NEIGHBORHOOD, AS IF THEY WERE TRYING TO TREAD LIGHTLY WITH HEAVY TIRES.

the pieced trees into yellow trucks, watched the trucks chipping the elms one slice at a time.

Susan put a hand on her stomach, checking

The bonsai was just like the lost elm in miniature. It even had moss at its base, moss that crept up the trunk just a little. Its tiny leaves spread out wide from its branches. When she opened the window, they made little rustling sounds.

Susan kept the tree for three weeks, carefully watering it once a day as the instruction card said, making sure it got at least five hours of sunlight and never experienced temperatures below forty degrees or above eighty-five. When the tiny leaves first started falling, she thought the little tree had confused the seasons. She started singing summer songs while she watered it each morning.

Summertime, she'd croon, warbling uncertain, *And the living is easy...?*

+++++

On the banks of the stream they strip naked, bashful at first, then daring as the chill of the water sets into their ankles. They follow the current, John picking his way across boulders, Susan curling her toes over rocks.

They stop beneath a tree on the bank. They lie on a bright patch of moss. They lie with their eyes closed and Susan makes lists in her head of everything she has to do at the end of the weekend while John tries to reach for the phone nestled snug in the bottom of his shoe. He catches himself and reaches for Susan's breasts instead. She stiffens at the feeling of his hands, cold against her cold skin. Then she remembers why they are here in the first place.

They make awkward love beneath the tree,

the exhilaration of it settling in only afterwards as they wade back to the tent, as they watch the water ripple around their ankles.

Susan glances down at her face staring up from underwater. It looks shadowy, tangled in her damp hair, and wild. She wonders if there is another her somewhere, a her that fits here, a her without a list or a car or a job, a her who doesn't flinch when her husband touches her breasts.

+++++

When, one week after they first began to fall, the leaves were still drooping, Susan went to the store for fertilizer. By the end of the second week, when all but a few leaves were gone, she began to talk to it.

Come on, little tree, she'd say, *don't be sad. Don't you like it in here?*

The leaves no longer rustled when she opened the window. Instead they hung, wilted and silent.

Don't die, she whispered to it every morning before going to bed.

One night she woke with a familiar cramped feeling, the familiar spots of blood, so small and so soon. So normal that, for a moment, she thought it was just her period. Half asleep, the familiar wave of relief that she'd felt each month all through

WHEN THE TINY LEAVES FIRST STARTED FALLING, SHE THOUGHT THE LITTLE TREE HAD CONFUSED THE SEASONS.

college and all through her twenties and half of her thirties washed over her. Not pregnant. Not pregnant. Thank god. Then she remembered.

In the morning, the tree's last leaf had fallen.

Three years before, vacationing, they'd driven down through the California summer. Dead trees lined the highways in rows, casting long leafless shadows over the naked cracked dirt: orchards parched white in the drought.

Susan could feel their dead eyes on her as she stared out the window, could feel the ghosts of them whispering as the car passed them by. They were angry in death, she thought; how could they not be?

John had just suggested that they try for a family. At age thirty-six after four years of marriage and six years of dating, with two good jobs between them and almost enough saved for a down payment on a house, it was not, Susan thought, an unreasonable suggestion.

Watching the trees whir past the window, Susan thought that they looked like bleached bones. They had the same languid quality as those Georgia O'Keefe skulls, like deeply dreaming creatures. But when they woke, she thought, they'd be treacherous. They'd have their revenge.

In the car, Susan gazed at John's profile, imagining a baby with a nose just like his, all crooked and bony and big. The thought made her laugh. John frowned at her, keeping his eyes on the road.

"What's so funny?" he asked.

"Nothing," she said. "Okay. Let's have a baby."

The smile he gave her was like looking at sunlight through deep green summer leaves.

John pressed his foot down on the gas, speeding up, putting the terrible dead stretch behind them.

She'd watched John's face shift when she told him, turning suddenly tired, turning suddenly old. She watched it wrinkle up, wilting into itself.

"Maybe this just isn't going to work for us," he said quietly, and beneath the words, Susan could hear the thought he wouldn't ever say: Maybe *you* just don't want it enough.

They'd always talked of wanting two, a boy and a girl—not a greedy amount, just enough to replace them. They'd name the girl Ellen for John's mother. They'd name the boy Fred for Susan's father. They'd raise them without Barbies or G.I. Joes or pink or blue or plastic or gender expectations. They'd give them toys made of natural materials—wood and wool and cotton and vegetable dye—so that they'd know what the real world felt like. They'd take them to the park and teach them how to push their swings higher and higher by pumping their legs. They'd teach them how to ride the bus, how to keep a vegetable garden, how to like gluten-free sugar-free cookies and dairy-less milk. They'd take them camping so they wouldn't be afraid, so they wouldn't feel the need to reach for cell phones, so they wouldn't worry about going a day without showers, so they'd know how to be in the woods. Their kids would be stronger than they were, and braver and wiser—more good.

As a child, Susan believed that babies grew out of the ground like daffodils. They waited, she thought, curled up like bulbs in the dark

y wouldn't
he need
wouldn't
showers,
woods.

They'd take them camping so they wouldn't
be afraid, so they wouldn't feel the need
to reach for cell phones, so they wouldn't
worry about going a day without showers,
so they'd know how to be in the woods.

They'd tak
be afraid
to reach
worry abo
so they'

underground, until spring when the light woke them and they dug their way out. She'd never been sure where she'd gotten the idea. From a children's cartoon? From her mother? She held onto it as long as she could, longer than she should have, until fifth grade Sex Ed. shocked her out of it with its cold Latin terms and tidy black and white maps of her insides.

She thought of those black and white maps, all the parts neatly labeled, leaving no room for error, no space for incompetence. She imagined rows and rows of little fetuses curled up bulb-like in the dark, a flowerbed of fetuses shriveling and dying, never alive, never waking up, abnormal, incompetent, victims of toxins and diseases and bodily failure.

John stopped holding her while they slept. She'd wake in the morning from dreams of infants growing up from cracked soil, scratching their ways through dead leaves. She'd wake in the morning facing the curve of his back as he cuddled the wall.

+++++

When evening comes, they build a fire and cook beans in a metal pan. John pares sticks, scraping bark down to wood flesh. Susan fumbles with the graham cracker wrappers. They laugh when their marshmallows catch on the flames, glowing and black on the outside. Susan blows her marshmallow out and traps it between crackers, watches it squishing, its charred brittle surface giving way to gooey insides.

John lays his head on her shoulder.

"This is nice," he says.

Susan thinks of the bonsai tree with its last fallen leaf, its tiny roots cut to perfect shape and size.

+++++

They'd left the dead tree on the windowsill for weeks. She stopped watering it, stopped singing to it, stopped looking at it. She didn't look at the space of sky in the window where the elm had been either.

One day, she came home and the little tree was gone. The aloe and the lucky bamboo had been moved one inch each to take up the bit of extra space again, as if the third tiny plant had never been there at all. John sat at the table with a bottle of wine and two plates of pasta.

"Let's get out of town," he said. "Let's go camping."

+++++

The night empties the world of its light as John and Susan sit by their shrinking fire, full and drowsy. Susan can still just distinguish the sky from the tree branches tangling above them. She feels enclosed, as if the world has shrunk to nothing but their fire and her eyes. The trees make noises in the breeze, their little creaks and rustles echoing through the eerie nighttime quiet.

39

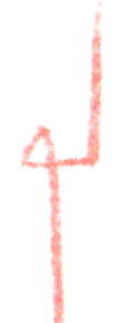

The giant fir trees frighten her. The oaks and the maples loom. They seem intent, aware, alive in a more than passive tree-like way. The fire, sinking into embers, pops within a burning piece of wood.

Soon there'll be no light at all, she thinks. She feels observed. There in the dark, a something watches them, waiting for the firelight to die. It sounds like a breath beside her ear. And it grows, surrounding.

At first, she thinks she is just imagining it. It seems not-quite-real. Then she feels John grip her hand, and she knows that if she is imagining, then so is he.

They sit together, silent, waiting, as the breath grows nearer, circling their campsite, making no footsteps, cracking no branches, rustling no leaves. The breathing sounds through the trees. It seems to come from all around them.

She feels a piece of metal in her palm.

"Take it," John says.

She moves her hand around the tiny blade. It glints in the embers' light, making her feel small, as well, and helpless—utterly unprepared for all these trees and all the creatures in them.

"What do we do?" she whispers.

"I don't know," John says, his voice sounding as tense as a string pulled too tight.

"Are we supposed to be quiet and wait for it to go or make noise and scare it?"

"I don't know," John says.

He rummages for his flashlight, finds it, flips it on. He creeps around the edge of their campsite, lighting the woods as he goes.

The breath continues, but louder now, almost breaking to a cry.

She sees the eyes across the fire, two bits of black, as blank and smooth as underwater stones, glinting.

She feels a scuttling inside her head, a momentary madness as she tries to read the eyes' intent. Do they want to eat her? Scare her? Are they just curious? She can't tell. They only glint and stare in their strange stony ways, giving her nothing she can understand. John doesn't see them as he sweeps his flashlight through the woods. Susan can't seem to move.

A wind rattles through the branches above them, sending needles falling. She can hear

IT SEEMS TO COME FROM ALL AROUND THEM.
THE BREATHING SOUNDS THROUGH THE TREES.

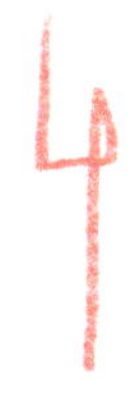

their pit-pats in the air. They fall in the embers and pop into flame, small and quick to burn.

She hears the something shuffling, the shifting of dead leaves. The breath moves closer. It smells of daffodils.

She is standing, the pan from dinner in her hand. She hits the pan with the knife, making a hard, metallic clang. She hits the pan again, again, and kicks the dying fire, sending sparks into the empty space where the empty eyes had been.

By the time she stops, the breath is gone, the trees are silent. John stares at her, surprised.

+++++

They don't speak as they douse the fire and retreat to their tent. Inside the nylon flap, they sit with their flashlight on.

"Do you think it will come back?" Susan asks, surprised at the hope that it will mixing in with the hope that it won't.

"I don't know," John says.

Susan listens for the sound of breath outside. She can still hear it, almost, as if it has lodged itself inside her ear.

Inside the tent, the woods feel far away. But for the rush of wind in the trees, they could imagine themselves back in their apartment.

"We should get some sleep," John says.

So they turn off the light and burrow deep into their sleeping bags.

In the woods, the little limbs creep, tiny feet rustling through the undergrowth, soft hands clutching at the ground, breathing and kicking the rhythms of branches on a windowpane. The trees whisper over the couple as they sleep and dream their people dreams. The last leaves dangle in their branches, sheltering the starlight, shadowing the moon. ⓑ

MISSED CONNECTIONS #6: FOUR-ALARM BLAZE IN MY HEART

Words by Joel Preston Smith

Artwork by Brianna Spencer

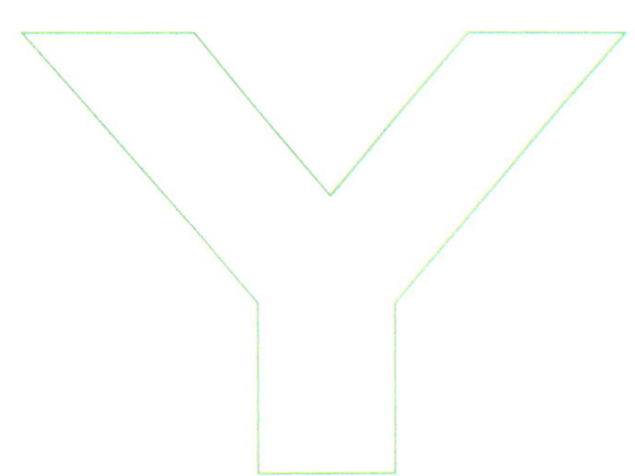

ou were distracted with work. I was shattered. I tried to get your attention but you were chopping out the windshield of the live news truck with an ax and threading a surprisingly flexible hose through the passenger window with your friends. I admit I admired you for your singular mindedness and what appeared to be inexhaustible stamina.

I was in the 2017 white Land Rover Range Rover parked directly behind you. It had (and still does) diamond-plate panels on the wing steps and halogen fog lights (not my idea but I won't go into that just now) bolted to the cowcatcher. I tried to turn them on to be helpful but I'm not sure you noticed, what with all the smoke pouring out the building, over the ladder truck with the telescoping hydraulic ladder that was five or so feet too short, making your important and daring work all the much harder I'm sure.

My youngest adopted daughter (12, adventurous, precocious, patriotic, curious and an environmentally concerned caffeine addict lol and just loves to meet new people) shot some HD video of you helping several very attractive and exceptionally friendly civilians from a nearby rental drag box springs and mattresses underneath the area where you or perhaps the incident commander believed the distraught person might land. I can Dropbox you a link if you like.

BTW I'm sorry your inflatable diving pod (couldn't find the exact name) wouldn't fully or partially inflate. What I realized, not for the first time, was that the failure of Bond Measure 38 meant a lot more than just a grassroots effort to replace flammable public housing with modern wetlands, allowing some inner-city youth to access a sustainable urban wilderness during day trips. It meant (in retrospect) the district's 19 racially integrated fire stations could not upgrade their outmoded and antiquated equipment or adequately re-accessorize.

Not that this is terribly relevant but it also meant that my youngest adopted daughter's middle school could not afford current social-sciences textbooks, which ultimately culminated in my child's recently having given an embarrassing World Geography oral report on the need for first-strike U.S. nuclear-missile capabilities against the Soviet Union when in fact that cruel and repressive regime collapsed more than 15 years ago (the school boiler also needs replaced, and Clarion is in the 'good' part of Irvington!). We all suffered as a consequence is my main point.

I cannot help but feel we failed you. Even though I personally voted for the measure and also talked my neighbor Clara into it, too. I knew this when I saw you sobbing into the sleeve of your Tactical Responder Parka. And then tearing off components of your OSHA-approved Personal Alert Safety System and throwing them at the reporters. BTW, I believe I have the GPS part. Should I just turn it into the nearest district headquarters, or possibly could I give it to you in person? If the latter, where would I find you? If you'd like to meet up for coffee, respond (for verification purposes) with the color of the blocked hydrant.

P.S. Are you all required to grow two days worth of razor stubble? If so, it's a municipal reg I can live with! ⓑ

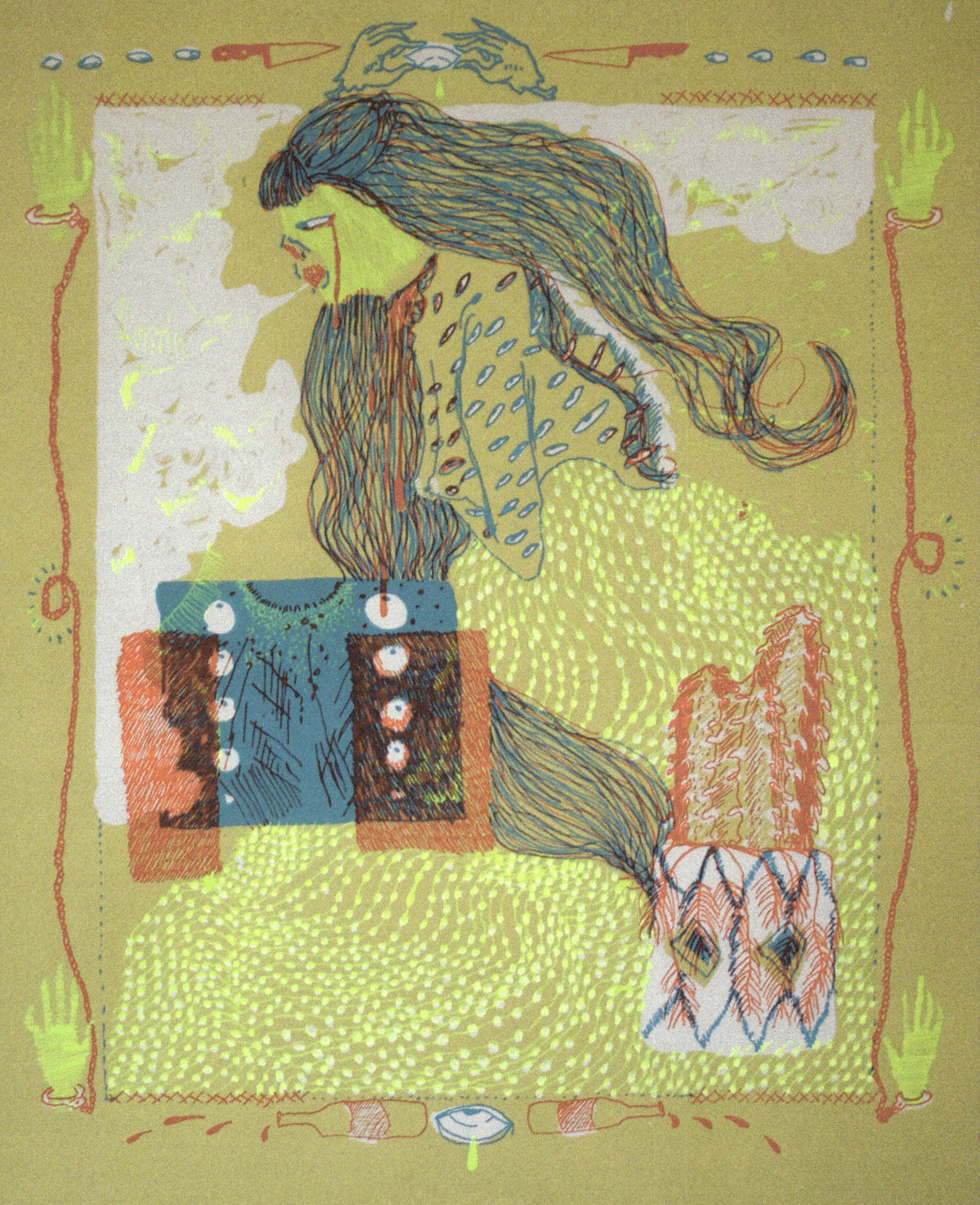

MADE BY BRUTAL BREASTS

Words by Craig Buchner
Artwork by Leslie Dorcus

Craig Buchner's fiction and poetry have been featured in *Tin House, The Baltimore Review, Hobart, The Cincinnati Review,* and many other literary journals. He is also the recipient of the AWP Intro Journals Award for his fiction. Although he was born and raised in the Adirondacks of New York State, Craig calls Portland, OR, home, where he lives with his wife and daughter.

To read more of his work, go to:
www.craigbuchner.com

rabbing the pregnancy test by the wrong end. First a solid pink line and a second coming into view. Kitchen shades half drawn. Light enough to see the future. But Wendy was walking into the living room, said nothing.

"This is exciting," I said. "We're excited. Right?"

I poured vodka into two tumblers. I liked good vodka; we only had bad vodka.

"Honeybear?"

Wendy didn't have the personality to celebrate, so I poured hers down the drain. In a couple weeks, our baby would be the size of a sweet pea. It was better Wendy didn't drink.

New Year's Eve at the Blue House Rooftop Lodge. Our babymoon. At the last minute my brother Ed said he'd pay the tab if he could join us. He had promised to keep to himself.

Decoration codfish—made of Portuguese porcelain—hung on the walls; the balcony overlooked downtown. Wendy was almost in her second trimester, and Ed asked about her nerves.

"She gets a cramp," I said, "and she's on her phone reading about somebody's miscarriage."

"That's good though, right?" Ed asked. "Everything's already happened to someone so there's no surprises."

I said, "What's good if everything you read ends in miscarriage?"

"What's good is right?" he asked, as if the

> # WHAT'S GOOD IF EVERYTHING YOU READ ENDS IN MISCARRIAGE?

question was one for the ages. But he was drunk.

Two bottles of white wine and two bottles of vodka, empty. We weren't alcoholics. But we were on vacation, and we drank like we were the real deal. If I knew the thing I'd become, maybe I'd have quit cold turkey.

"I should check on her," I said.

Wendy watched Netflix on her iPad. Binging a show about a stalker who dates the woman he stalks until he finds out she's sleeping with another man. Wendy had been drawn in like a wolf to raw meat. She gave me *that* look.

"What'd you read now?" I said.

"I'm worried."

Wendy pulled up her shirt. Her stomach was relatively flat, a few dark hairs sprouting around her belly button. She cupped her left tit. "See?"

From the side angle, it looked like a nipple the size of a pea had grown off the tip of her original nipple.

"Is it cancer? Be honest."

Wendy was vegan, but on trips like this she ate cheese and eggs and poured real cow's milk into her coffee at breakfast. You'd have to ingest straight rBST for a century to grow a third nipple, I thought.

Wendy inspected her other tit. "Quit staring."

"I barely looked."

I grew up Roman Catholic. When I was little, my grandmother told me all Christians were good people. And she said to always be a good boy and always tell the truth. Now that we were having our own kid, I wanted to teach it about faith. It was the practical thing to do. That was why we chose Buddhism. It was like Christianity without all the bad stuff, I had joked, but I had no idea. I only had enough of an understanding of Buddhism under my belt to know I should choose a meditation mantra—*I always have a chance to do good, I always have a chance to do right*—and repeating it throughout the day helped clear my thoughts.

"It's probably just a skin tag," I said, staying positive. "But even if it is a nipple you can get it removed. I don't even care though. Don't sweat it."

Wendy wasn't listening. She squeezed the skin between her fingers, and the end bulged bright and red.

"Don't milk it," I said. "It'll pop."

"I'm sure someone on the Internet's grown a third nipple. But now you're going to say, if you look hard enough you can find anything on there. And I'm going to say, that means I'm right. And you're going to get mad at me again."

I took her face between my hands. "I would never," I said, and kissed her right eye lid.

"Then you'll be annoyed," she said, looking at me with one closed eye.

"Getting warmer."

I didn't tell Ed about the third nipple. Instead I told him she was feeling better, and he poured two more drinks to celebrate.

"To the tiny victories," he said, holding up his glass.

"*Kanpai*," I said, and clinked mine against his.

Tomorrow we might have all the answers to life's questions, but tonight we stayed awake past midnight and watched the fireworks from the balcony, content with all we didn't know. A brocade crown filled the air with big hanging breaks of gold, slowly fading to right us. But

largest child care company. Elevator doors boasted vibrant images of blissful boys and girls and theys, their hands coated in bright paint and glitter, and happy teachers teaching. An invention of childhood straight from the minds of mostly single, childless marketing managers.

Similarly, I never liked kids enough to want my own—until now.

Wendy texted during a sales meeting. She wrote, *Don't judge me.*

I held my phone beneath the conference table so only I could see the screen. *Why?*

Can you get chicken strips on your way home?

Who does vegan strips? I nodded at the Head of Marketing, who carried on about his editorial calendar. He, like the rest of us, did not have children. But we all spoke as if we knew exactly what parents needed in a childcare provider.

I mean, analog strips. I had this memory today and now I want chicken. You don't know what it's like being pregnant.

I thought of my mantra, but between the meeting and the texting I couldn't concentrate. I snapped off a quick reply: *What about the shitty diseases you say I'll get from real meat?*

The doctor said to listen to my body. So...

Everyone in the room nodded; I nodded

TOMORROW WE MIGHT HAVE ALL THE ANSWERS TO LIFE'S QUESTIONS, BUT TONIGHT WE STAYED AWAKE PAST MIDNIGHT AND WATCHED THE FIREWORKS FROM THE BALCONY, CONTENT WITH ALL WE DIDN'T KNOW.

beautiful things never last.

Work was impossible. I spent my days at the corporate headquarters of the country's

along with them. *Did you Google it first?*

Fuck right off.

I stood in line at Burger King. I loved chicken

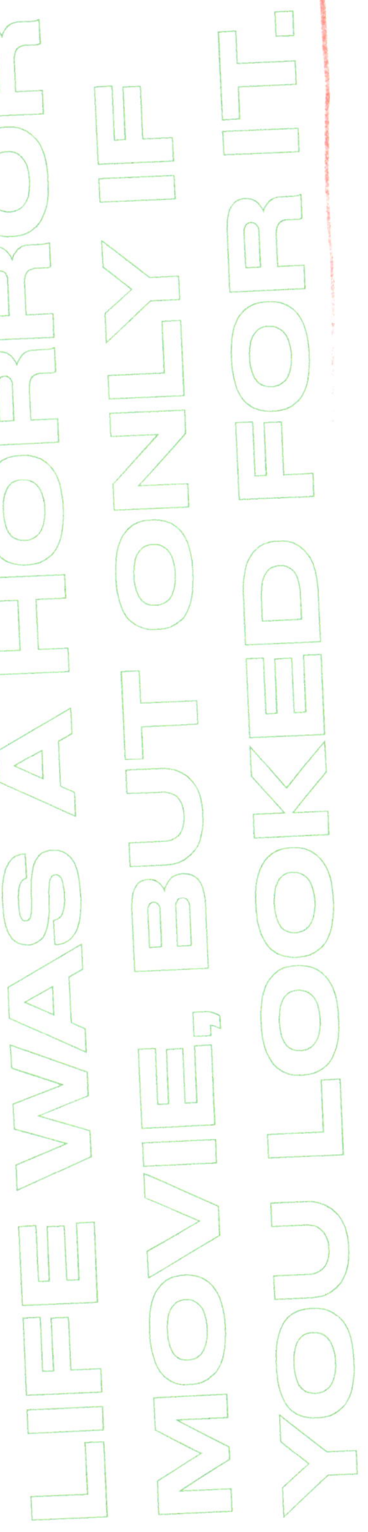

tenders as a kid, but as an adult I watched a documentary about how they were made. Lab-created super chickens with mammoth bodies, like gargantuan dogs really, except sixteen sets of wings and no heads. Life was a horror movie, but only if you looked for it.

I'd heard women had worse cravings, but I was the accomplice to this one. Wendy didn't need authentic chicken fingers, and we knew it. They say pregnancy brain is a real thing, and this was another case of all those chemicals blasting through her body. A better plan, I told myself, was to pick up a sweet potato bowl with extra avocado from a food cart. I stepped out of line but knocked into him—the CEO at my company. Duane Everett Earp.

"Sir," I said, "I work for you. On the twelfth floor. I recognize you from your photo."

"Well, howdy," Duane Everett Earp said. He stood a few inches shorter, but he was built like an MMA flyweight. Arms striped with thin muscles and thick veins. I'd never seen him without his sport jacket.

"Are you here for dinner?" I asked.

"I'll tell you what, my wife can run circles around half the chefs in this town, but when I need comfort food, I come here. Honest to god. I can remember eating the French fries in the backseat of my momma's station wagon. Just the smell brings her back."

"I've got the same memory," I lied. "But chicken tenders. They're for my wife though. Pregnancy craving."

"Expecting? You work at the right company for that, and I'll tell you, businesses like this one here inspire me," he said. "We grow up and get big kid jobs, but there's something about this food we can't outgrow."

"I'd say you have more than a big kid job." I didn't know what else to say.

"Looks like you're up, partner."

I ordered Wendy's chicken tenders and large fries.

Duane Everett Earp ran a two-billion-dollar business, and I was in therapy because I drank too much. But here we were, occupying the same space. The clerk pulled boxes of hot fast food from the warming tray. I looked beyond her to the French fry bin. Thousands of perfectly cut fries glowing golden under a heat lamp with white salt reflecting like diamond powder.

The cashier handed me my bag, but Duane Everett Earp stopped me.

"Do you mind? I haven't had one of their fingers in eons."

"You want one of my wife's fingers?" I asked, confused.

"If it's not a bother."

Duane Everett Earp reached into the bag and pulled out the box, choosing one delicately fried chicken tender. His large white teeth sliced through the meat, and he pushed the rest between his pink lips, sucking off the fry and yellow grease. A red pain boiled in my gut. He licked the corner of his lips. Slick tongue lingering.

"Nothing beats a freebie," he said.

I could not remember the mantra. Screw the mantra. I had an urge to bite into his neck. Let his loose body fall like a sack of old meat. There was something primal inside me.

Our home changed. Baby stroller, baby books, car seat, and toys. We baby-proofed all the cabinet doors in the kitchen with baby blue latches, and Wendy's torpedo belly rubbed the counter as she reached for a water glass.

"How you doing? I mean, your body. You okay?"

"Never not tired," she said, panting slightly. "I never thought it would be easy, but I had no idea what it meant to have a body until now. Just moving takes effort."

"I can imagine," I said, but I couldn't. "Let's take a load off. Take a nap?"

We got into bed, and I rubbed a circular pattern on her belly, kissed the top of the mound, and then kissed her navel, then her underwear. Her crotch smelled of urine; I didn't care. Tiny hairs poked through the weave, like the flesh of a baby cactus.

I closed my eyes and listened. Inhaled and listened. Cheek nuzzled into her thigh; I could take that nap, but I kissed the cotton, and she let out the smallest moan. I kissed the inner band. Dark, thick hair flaring from beneath. Playfully I deployed to her thigh, but the hair continued.

So furry, I thought, and she said, "Don't stop."

But I did. Short patches of brown hair on each leg—like tufts from the belly of a wild boar. How had I not noticed? I tried to focus. The fabric and the orgasmic spots. But the hair on her thighs tickled my neck, and I got a strand in

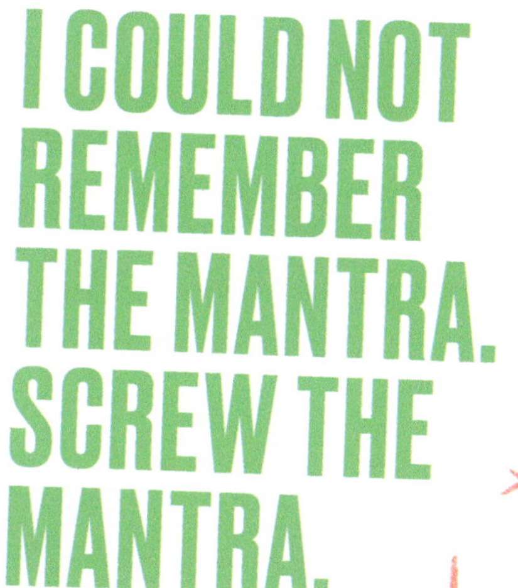

my mouth, pulling it from my lips.

"What's wrong?" Wendy stared down her chest.

Peering up between her legs, I said, "What do you mean?"

"You stopped. Keep going."

"Okay," I said. "I'm just breathing."

She laid back and said, "You can fuck me if you want to."

I said, "Maybe that's better," yanking more hair from my mouth.

Wendy rolled onto her hip, but I was soft, and it was hard to get started. She tugged my face to her tit.

"What's that?"

She said, "It's just that skin tag."

But another stripe of fur like a half-moon had grown across the top of her belly. Dark and bushy. I couldn't help but think of my own body hair. Like tendrils. The pubes and thigh and calf and butt hair I shed every time I sat on the toilet or showered or slept without underwear. Hairs lost to the most intimate spaces. She had always been different. Smooth and clean. Elevated beyond my own beastness. But now this.

"Is that normal?" I asked.

"Do you want to Google it?" she said, smirking.

"I'm serious."

"Nothing will happen to the baby, I promise."

"Why would your hair hurt the baby?"

"What hair? I'm talking about your dick. Is that what you're worried about? Body hair?"

"Wendy," I said, and reached for her hand. Her delicate, smooth hands—all that remained hairless. "I was just saying there's a lot of it, and I wasn't sure if that was normal or not."

"I think I want to stop," she said.

"I'm sorry," I said. "I just didn't know if you knew."

"It's my fucking body, Homer. Of course I know."

I searched online for the cause. Women in forums wrote about their own experiences, the rapid hair growth. The hair usually fell out after birth. I thought of Wendy in bed. Sleeping now. Her cheek on her pillow. Her belly, the skin taut, and roots at the bottom of every single hair follicle. Blood feeding each one of them, and every single hair sprouting like a single blade of grass. All that hair pushing up through her skin breaking the surface to jacket her entire belly and arms and back. A dark, dense hide. Wendy's fur. It seemed unimaginable.

Trivia night at the Basement Pub meant sitting through an hour of impossible questions. It was the same gang as always: Me, Sandowski, and Gary. But this week we let two college kids join *Bling Kong Lives*. We never won the twenty-five-dollar voucher, but we put on like we did. The college kids looked at us with admiration, but after a few wrong answers, they left the bar.

"Millennials can't commit to shit," Gary said.

"Not like us," Sandowski said.

I said, "You both have kids, how hairy did your wives get during pregnancy?"

"What do you mean hairy?" Gary asked.

I wished I'd said something funny to change the subject, but I didn't want to make things weird.

"Body hair," I said. "Like thick body hair."

Gary and Sandowski looked at one another. "You mean 'cause she can't see where she's shaving with her belly and all?" Gary asked, and

A DARK, DENSE HIDE. WENDY'S FUR. IT SEEMED UNIMAGINABLE.

Sandowski said, "Hair in the usual spots, I guess. Like Gary said."

"Like fur. I wouldn't say it's gross, but I just wasn't sure what's normal and you know, what's abnormal."

Gary said, "What do you mean fur? Fur, like a pelt?"

"Sure," I said.

"A pelt of what?" Sandowski asked. "You mean pelt, like p.e.l.t.? Like the definition of pelt, pelt?"

They were both over ten-years married, so maybe I was thinking of things the wrong way. Or maybe they forgot on purpose.

"Forget it," I said.

"I'm not sure I can," Sandowski said.

"Next round's definitely on you, Homer."

It did not end with chicken strips. The week after, Wendy wanted corn dogs, and now hamburgers. Animalistic urges.

Naked, Wendy stared at her laptop, pillows propping her up in bed. She reached for a handful of fries from a greasy bag and wedged them into her mouth. One landed on the sheets.

"Napkin?" I asked.

"Starving," she grunted.

Months earlier she would've crucified me for spilling food, but I returned to her with a plate.

"You uncomfortable?"

"Overheating," she grunted.

Her large breasts hung over her enormous belly, with our baby's legs and arms swiping within. Nipples poking out new tufts of hair. Her entire stomach now covered in fur, armpit hair flaring from the creases. All of it somehow seemed unnatural. But like a mother chimpanzee, she sat naked and hairy, and she hand-picked crumbs from her own body.

"You're making a mess," I said.

She looked at me, the same foul stare I got when I drank too much, but she didn't speak. Instead a rumble escaped her body.

THPPTPHTPHPHHPH.

This squealing flatulence sliced through any other distraction. Yet, she held my gaze.

"Did you just... fart?" I asked.

"Fell out," she said, slow and thick, like she spoke the words through water.

When she finished, she quickly fell asleep. Around her snoring, I cleaned the discarded wrappers and pulled the blanket all the way up to the sprouts of hair on her jawline. I kissed her singular eyebrow; and she snorted. Dreaming, her arms and legs flinched, as if in chase. I had no idea of what, so I imagined all the

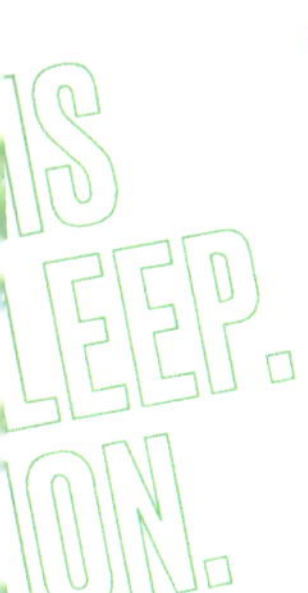

possibilities. A jackal charging down a rabbit. A horse breaking across a field. A tiger leaping for a gazelle. A dog fetching a limp pheasant. Maybe even Wendy, black coat of fur bristling, racing on all fours after a feral cat, its terrified yellow eyes swelling as Wendy snapped her mighty jaws into its weak, poor body. The crack of bone at the end. But then she stopped: arms and legs. Motionless in sleep. Silence was her perfection.

The idea of failure was something I talked about weekly with Monirée, my therapist. I didn't know much about Monirée except her office was too dark because the 20-watt bulb in the lamp in the corner was always failing.

In her quiet trust-me voice, she said, "Tell me about your week, Homer. Don't leave anything out."

I set my palm against my chin, like I was giving it incredible thought.

"Great week," I said.

"Good." Her eyebrows bounced. "And your job?"

"Great."

"Positive," Monirée said. "And your drinking?"

"Dry as a bone," I said, which was mostly true now that Wendy's due date was closing in.

"Living the best version of me."

"Your eyes look red," she said, then nodded as if to confirm. "Did you say you have allergies?"

I said, "Not much sleep with Wendy peeing all night. Everything pushes on her bladder."

Monirée wrote something in her notepad, but only said, "And how's that?"

I reached my arms over my head. I wasn't stretching; I didn't know what to do with my hands. We looked into one another's eyes. I looked away because I was doing it again, thinking I failed before I started.

"How is 'us'?" I asked.

"If that's what you want to talk about."

"We're changing. But it's good."

She didn't jot anything down; she didn't nod; she just said, "Changing how?"

"How we communicate. That stuff."

Monirée smiled. "Is that it then? You had a great week at work, you're not drinking, and things are good with your wife?"

It wasn't *it*; I could go on all session dodging her, or I could just tell her.

I said, "I'm getting hung up on how Wendy looks, but I think that's normal. Is that normal?"

"It's a lot to take in," she said, "with a baby growing inside of her. Do you feel left out?"

I said, "I don't do much, you know, in terms of helping the baby right now. So, yeah, maybe I feel like my job's over."

"But your next job is beginning. And she'll need to feel like you're committed, right? Not just to her but to them."

"But what about the hair?" I asked. "I think we're getting off topic."

It took me an hour to bring it up, but I knew our session was almost over. I wanted to talk about it, or I'd drown the problem back down inside me.

"What hair?"

"The pelt," I said. "Her entire body. Is that normal for pregnant women?"

"I'm not really sure. I'd assume some hair growth would be normal, considering everything she's going through." Then she asked, "Did you Google it?"

Weeks leading up the delivery, we talked in grunts and groans and mumbles and snorts. The toilet and bathtub were covered in her hair, and I vacuumed the living room daily. Piles of loose hair everywhere. Wendy slept fourteen and sixteen hours a day, and when she woke, she would wait at the back door until I opened it for her. She paced for a few minutes in the backyard, coming back inside panting.

"You feeling okay?"

"Uh."

Wendy drank water straight from the faucet, then got back into bed.

The Internet did not help, and the mantra could not bring us back.

Last New Year's Eve on the rooftop deck, Ed and I traded stories of childhood. After midnight and firecracker-drunk, we remembered winter days without power, remembered all the lamps our mother had bought after the divorce, remembered the hole in the station wagon floor—able to see the world beneath our feet as we drove, like we were princes on a flying carpet.

Ed said, "I used to have a cash cup in my room."

"From when you worked at Subway?"

"Mom would steal money out of it to pay her credit card bills. I had a hundred IOUs."

I closed my eyes, and I could see that claustrophobic house on the corner of Midline Road. Unfinished sheet rock walls. Cracked lamp shades. Empty cupboards. The stack of orange and yellow notices on the kitchen table like they were party napkins.

We stood against the railing. "Too bad Subway didn't pay more," I said, and elbowed him. "So you're to blame I grew up poor?"

The fireworks finale had ended long ago, but every so often, an orphan shot streamed across the night. A bloodshot pop and blue gasp of smoke. From the terrace we looked over the

city and smirked at something far away. In the distance or the past. Maybe we had escaped.

"In a fucked-up way, you're not wrong," Ed said. "Now drink up while you got it. Because you'll be on baby watch soon enough"

A car drove into the alleyway below us. There was only enough room to drive in and reverse out, but the car tried to turn around. A ten-point turn until it was stuck. The driver opened the door and inspected any clearance he still might have. He lit a cigarette, and then he walked away. Someplace was more important than this problem.

"Could you ever leave?" I asked. The retreating man had no idea what was ahead of him in the alley, but he headed straight into the shadows. "Like dad?"

"That's why I don't want kids."

"Why's that?"

Ed said, "So I don't have to find out."

Wendy nested in bed with a body pillow clutched between her legs. Going on sixteen hours of sleep. I posted up in the living room. The baby could come any day. I wondered what that day would be like. A stranger in our family. We had no idea who we were getting. We had all the information about everything we could ever need, yet tiny limbs of fear crawled over of skin. I needed levity, but I was on strict

sobriety. A glass of ice-cold water to ground me into the present.

I watched *Animal Planet*, a show about dogs. A golden retriever named Lulu padded a bed on a square of newspapers. Her belly sagged, nipples red and protruding. I don't remember if I fell asleep or not, but I remember seeing Wendy's sad eyes, like Lulu's, then waking to her yelling from the room. Labor, I thought. She

sat straight up in bed, grabbing at her thighs. It seemed like it happened so fast. But I had a chance to do right.

"What is it? Tell me what's wrong."

Her speech was thick and sloppy. "My leg," she groaned.

"Did your water break? Should I look it up?"

For nine months they were together, mother and passenger. And though I had done my part in the beginning, I was back again.

"Cramp," she said.

"What?"

"M'okay."

"Are you okay? Did you say you're okay?"

"Cramp. Leave."

I did not go back to sleep. I laid in the dark beside her, listening to her breath. Our child was under the surface of her skin. Waiting for its moment. Waiting to grow and learn and have its own mantra. Waiting to love us, hate us, run from us, and fly back to us. All of its life swept through my head. That was my trial.

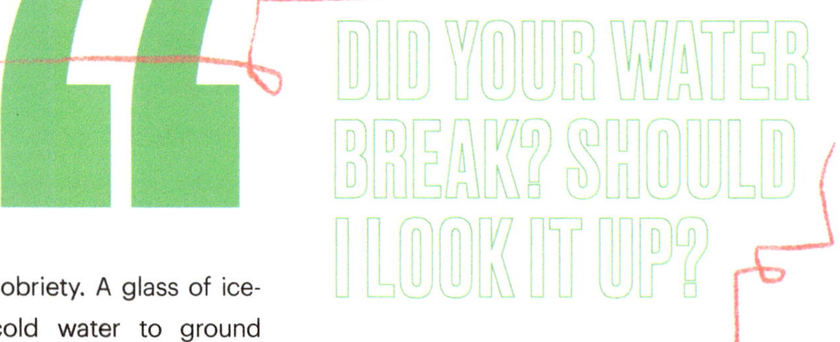

Even the real thing flashed by. The drive to the hospital. The nurses. Our doctor. Twenty-hours.

In the delivery room, I can remember her legs covered in sweat. All of the furniture was another shade of blue, except the pine veneer

NOT HUMAN, BUT ALIVE. THE SMELL OF NEW BIRTH. WILD-HAIRED AND UNRULY.

cabinets. The doctor wore circular glasses like John Lennon, and Wendy was moaning and crying, and someone—a nurse—calmly, slowly said, "Now." A tiny cone-shaped head emerging her, glazed in gore. I cut the cord.

Wendy nuzzled the child. The waste from her own body on its head. Not human, but alive. The smell of new birth. Wild-haired and unruly. They were skin to skin in the bed, and I stood only a few feet away, but the gap looked like a million, million miles through my eyes. There was one future that would never begin for me, and this was the new future. I knew I needed to get to them, but we had been so distant. Speaking entirely different languages. One human, one animal. A moment of rage stopped me. Red spots blurring the curves of sight, and me and rage saw her, our child—a daughter. Pale and

wrinkled, she was frantic until Wendy showed her love; she licked her forehead. Forget all the hair and gore, it was kindness. It was pure. And I needed that; I needed *her*.

The room was the dark night in that dark alley, and I was that stranger walking into the shadows. I could not see into the unknown, and I was afraid, but a crying joy replaced that fear— this was nature's revelation. The way Wendy's fingers traced her face. I wanted everything between them. They brought me to my knees, as if in prayer. If they asked me, I would kill for them and then lick their perfect heads clean. ⬤

Following spread: Alyson Provax, 2019

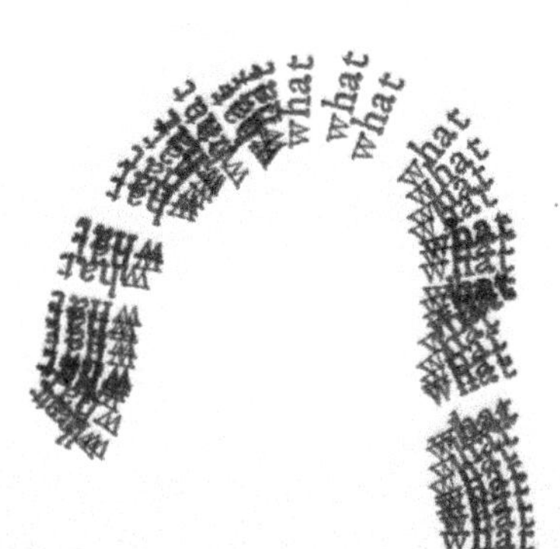

what what what what
what
what

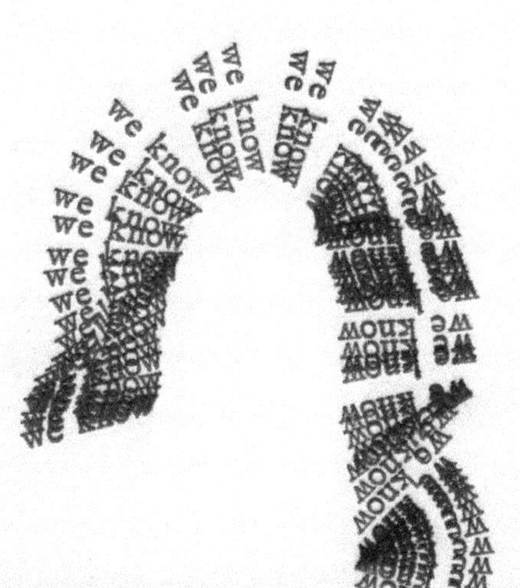

we know

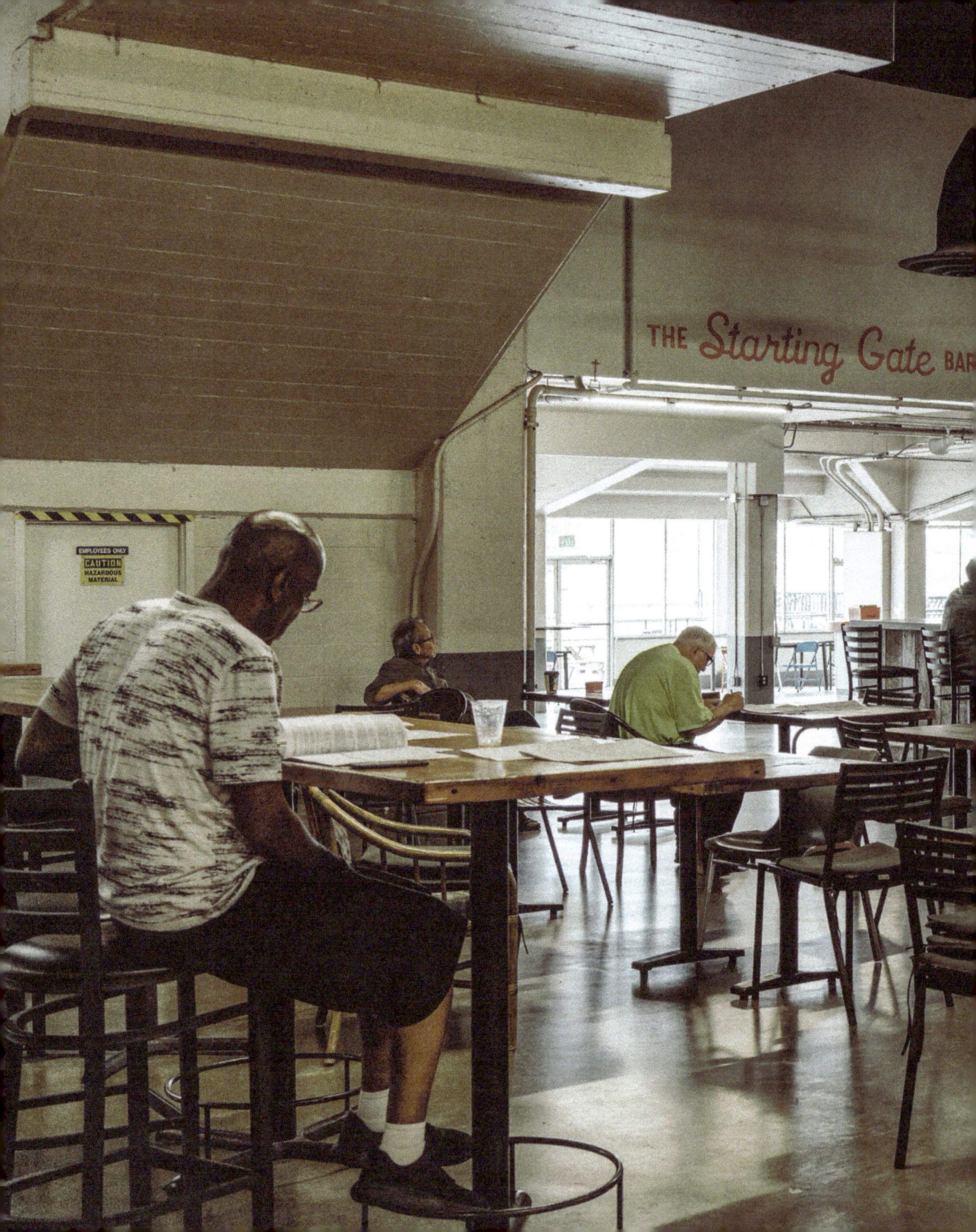

THE Starting Gate BAR
EMPLOYEES ONLY
CAUTION
HAZARDOUS
MATERIAL

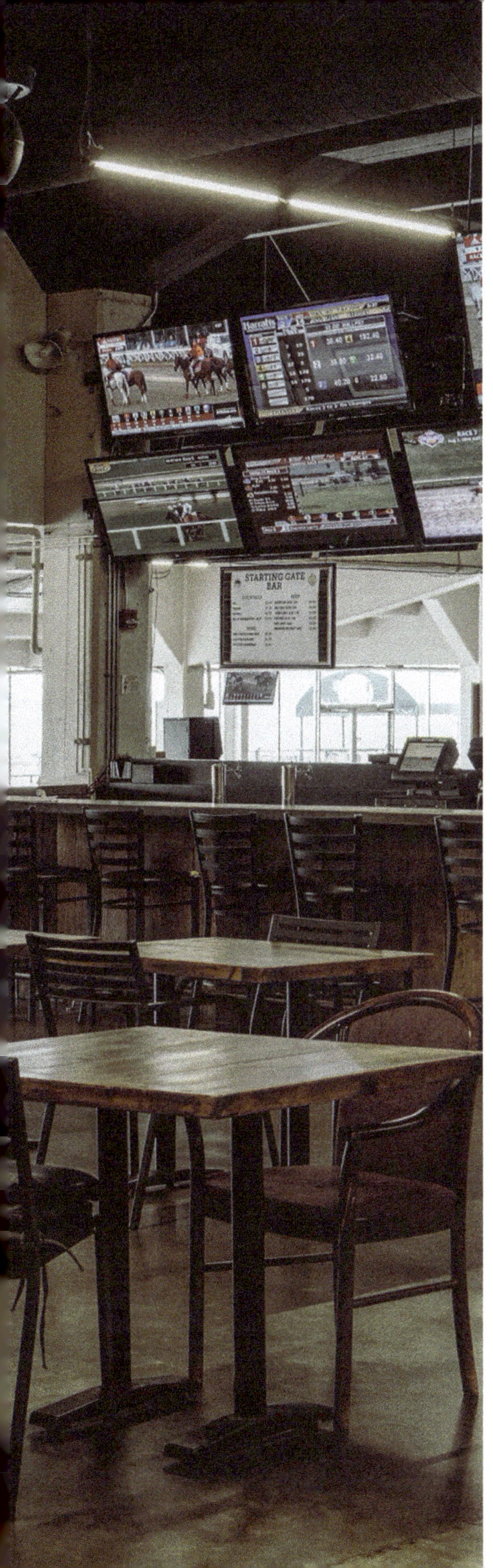

FINAL CALL FROM PORTLAND MEADOWS

Words by Rich Perin

Artwork by Hattie Watson

Rich Perin is mostly invisible. His short story collection, *The Last Payphone On The West Coast*, was published in 2019.

Since 1946, Portland Meadows served as Oregon's premier horse racing track. In the spring of 2019, it was announced that operations would cease by the year's end.

Portland Meadows was on its last legs with little left on the bones, the wrecking ball and bulldozers scheduled to appear in a few months. It had been on the downside for years, repairs delayed then abandoned, and what persisted aged ungracefully like weathered plastic. Off-track betting remained in the betting hall, but there were only a few gamblers trying their luck, maybe a dozen, the hardest of the hardcore. And although the indoor smoking ban was a decade old, somehow the betting hall still held a haze, as if fifty years of gambler cheers and grief collected, shrouding the air like ghosts.

I didn't plan to take my girlfriend's little brother to the horse track. He was a recent college graduate from New York, his first visit to the west coast. Holly had her suggestions. "Show him a Portland thing," she said. "Maybe a hike through Forest Park. Or check out some brew pub or food cart pod. Bicycle to a dispensary. Whatever. But don't take him to Powell's. I want to be the one that shows Powell's."

None of these suggestions appealed to me. I've lived here for too long and such activities rank as tourist. But what's old to me is new to the visitor and, besides, this was as an opportunity to bond with one of Holly's siblings.

But when he, Nicolas, ambled out of the airport arrivals gate I immediately knew the standard tourist affair was no longer on the table. He wasn't paying attention to where he was walking, his eyes and thumbs were locked on his smartphone screen. His face was smooth, neatly hedged of manicured mustache and matching sideburns. A tattoo of a butterfly landing on a tropical flower colored a forearm. He wore a striped shirt tucked into crisp jeans that were rolled above his ankles, revealing striped socks and pristine sneakers. I waved to draw his attention, but he was too busy pecking at the screen in his hand. I saw this as a dare to broaden the young man's horizons.

A text alert chimed from my phone, but I left it in my pocket. I approached and walked alongside Nicolas for a bit to measure his gait. He was a little taller than me, fit but gym fit. "Ahoy, Nicolas, right?"

"Yes," he said, turning to me but his phone still out and ready. "You must be Rich. I was just texting you."

"You don't say."

"Thanks for picking me up."

"No trouble, no trouble at all. Holly is excited to see you. She'll meet us later, when she finishes work."

"Sounds good. Until then, I'm all yours."

+++++

We were along Columbia Blvd, on top of a levee that divided the tarmac from the Columbia River, cruising the low speed limit. I was driving a 1972 Ford Galaxie 500, a mean weight of old American steel, black paint aged into patina, but the big engine true, tuned to an understated growl, ready to pounce and roar. A jet airliner swooped in for a landing only a few hundred feet above, its engines drowning Nicolas's voice.

"What was that?" I asked.

The old-fashioned seat belt, which was only a lap belt, made Nicolas nervous. It wasn't frayed, but the buckle looked rusty. One of Nicolas' hands gripped the door's arm rest, the other pressed down against the leather bench seat. "So, really, like, we're really going to the racetrack? Shouldn't we, um, drop off my luggage?"

I explained that Portland Meadows was nearby, and we wouldn't be in this part of town again. "Besides," I added, "Holly might meet us there after she finishes work."

"Holly goes to the racetrack?"

"Not often," I said. "Kentucky Derby, stuff like that. Baccarat is more of her game."

"I didn't know she gambled."

I thought Nicolas would pick up that I was joking but realized I needed to dial it back. I didn't want to weird him out too much. "She's not some kind of fiend, crouched over video poker," I reassured. "Baccarat is a very classy game."

Nicolas saw a fast food restaurant, said he was hungry, and suggested fries at the drive-thru.

"Nonsense," I responded. "There's a bar at the

track and we'll get some tater-tots to tide you over until dinner. We're eating out tonight. Trust me, you'll need an empty stomach. You like Ukrainian food? I sure could go for some dumplings."

+++++

The Meadows parking lot was enormous, big enough to accommodate several drive-in movies. I circled the expanse, parked the Galaxie in the front row, next to the entrance. The racetrack was a place of rare stillness in the city, no trees to rustle, no birds or bugs, the only thing showing signs of life was the giant neon galloping horse at the top of the entrance, its lights clicking on and off.

The glass doors at the entrance were greasy, an appropriate introduction for the bleak foyer. Its 20th century carpet had all plush and color grounded out. The drywalls were decorated with blanched photos and old paintings of horses and dignitaries, probably

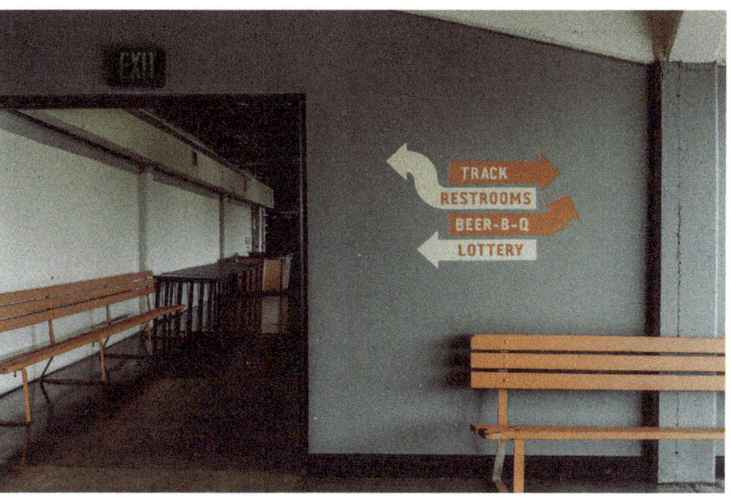

the only place on Earth that remembered their existence. A quick turn revealed the betting hall. It resembled a Greyhound bus station with its concrete floor and utilitarian columns to lean on, but instead of ticket windows there were betting windows, and throughout the hall an army of televisions broadcasted races from all over. The few gamblers were scattered around, all solitary, all male, middle-aged and older, looked sheepish as if they should be elsewhere. They chewed numbers, squinted worries, looked to the televisions for the latest odds, with betting slips flapping from polo shirt pockets.

Once, in more popular times, Portland Meadows offered a choice of several bars, even a Members Club. But now it could only sustain one bar at the north end of the building. Nicolas and I walked through the betting hall, then an empty video poker room, and found the empty bar and its bar tender who looked asleep. "Just resting my eyes," she said without opening them, hearing our approach. "What can I get for you fellas?" I ordered domestic beer, tater-tots, and jalapeno poppers, then we made our way back and sat at the unattended horseshoe bar. That old, wooden, chipped bar carried decades of hope and fade, and it sat in the middle of the betting hall, the epicenter of all the televisions, the best place to soak in the action.

"I thought there would be horses here," said Nicolas. "And maybe I'd get a selfie with one."

"Last live race was six months ago," I said. "Most tracks, outside of the big ones, are more about the simulcast," and I pointed my finger around the room, to the circumference of televisions. "Come on, eat, drink, then we'll

61

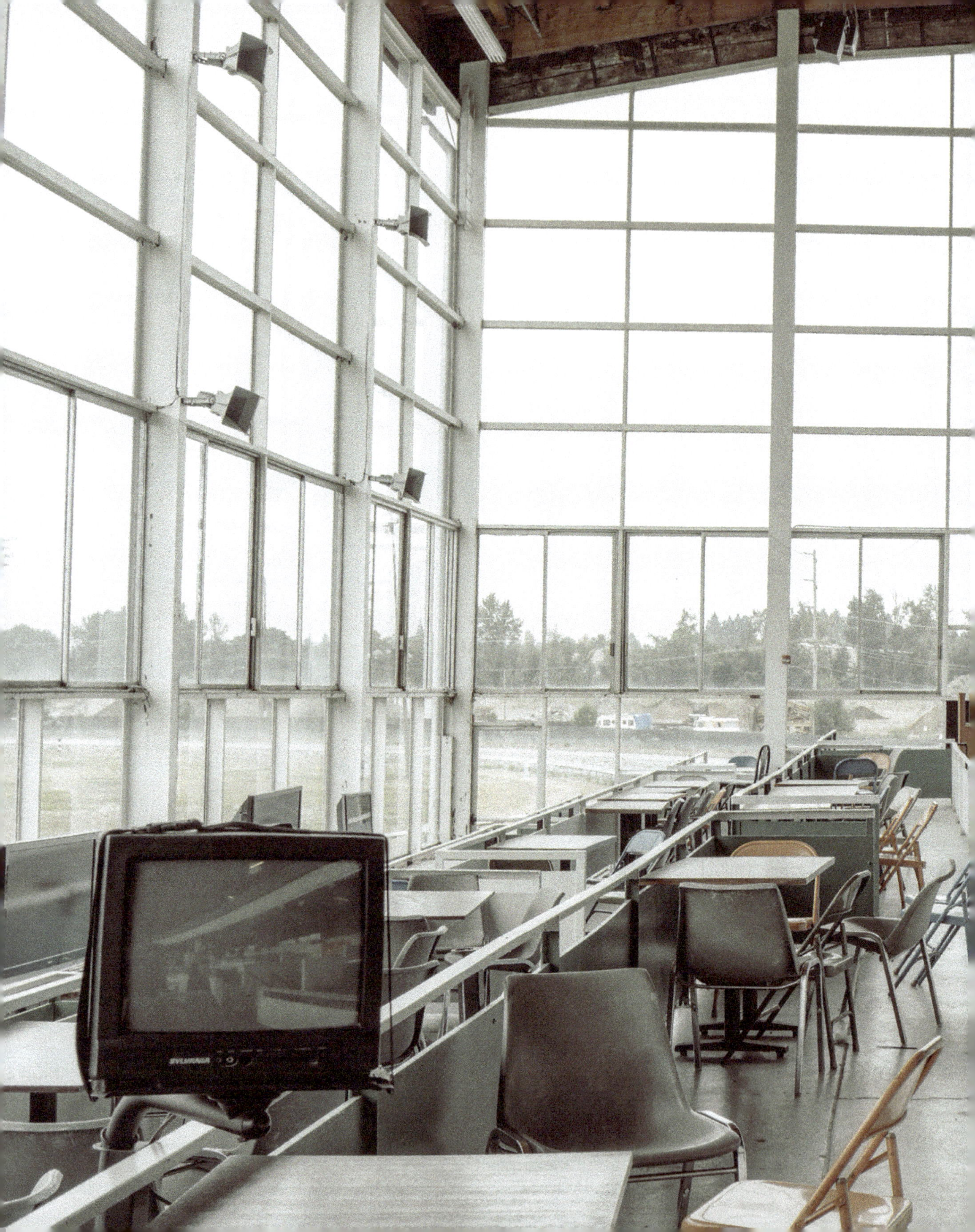

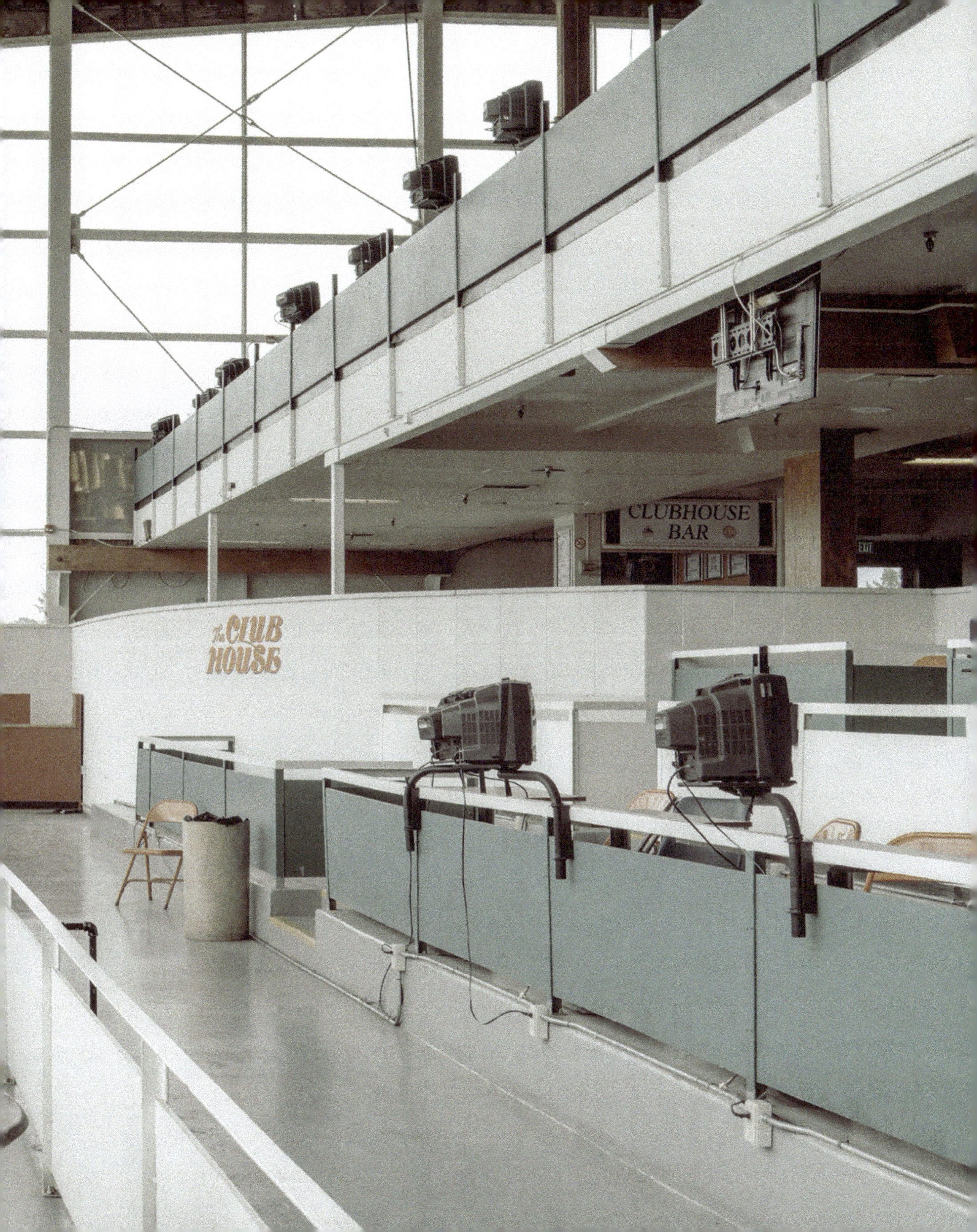

CLUBHOUSE BAR
EXIT
The CLUB HOUSE

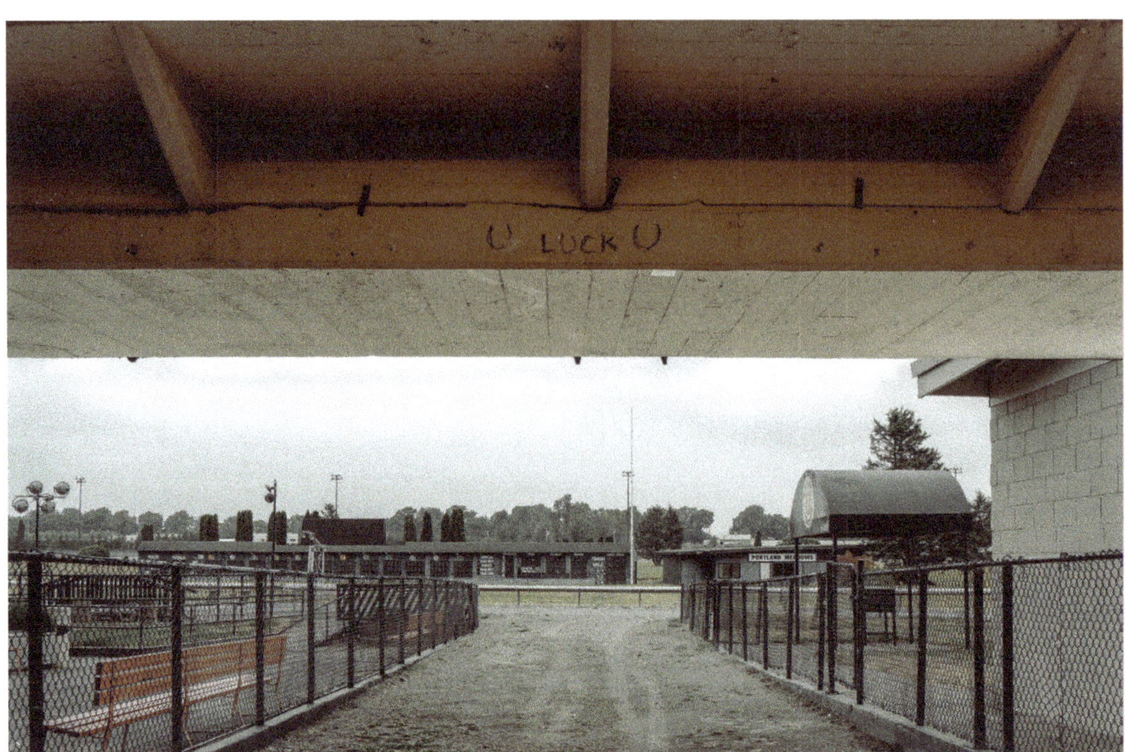

place a bet. Next race at Saratoga is up. That's your neck of the woods. You have insider information."

Nicolas bit into a jalapeno popper and burnt his tongue. "Hot, hot!" he shouted, gulped beer, then swished it around like mouthwash.

"That's the spirit," I said. "I'll get another round. See that screen," nodding to the one in front of us, "that's Saratoga. Let me know if any of the horses float your boat."

I returned with a pitcher of beer and extra sour cream for the poppers. Nicolas' glass was near empty and he was still swishing beer around his mouth. "See any horse you like?" I asked.

He finished off his beer. "Well, yes, actually. But I don't understand all the numbers, the odds, the trifectas... none of it. I found an app we can download that...."

"Don't worry about that shit. We'll just pick winners. What's the horse?" I asked as I looked up to the flat screen.

"By Jove Anchovy."

"What?"

"By Jove Anchovy. Number 12."

It appeared on the screen, a steel grey, prancing around behind the other horses, very excitable. "Why number 12?" I asked.

"My grandfather liked anchovies. Always had anchovies on his pizza. And he smoked a pipe, and that horse has a smoky look to it."

"Sounds wise to me. Let's drop twenty bucks each. On the nose, as they say."

"Forty dollars, excellent!"

"No, twenty, each. There's no holding hands in horse racing."

"I just thought that if we pooled our money together, we'd get a higher rate of return."

"Jesus. It doesn't work like that. Trust me, drink some beer, take in the Oregon air, relax and enjoy the anticipation before the race." We placed our bets at the sole betting window that was open.

By Jove Anchovy was second to last coming into the final turn. Nicolas slumped. "I think our horse is a dud," he said.

"Hold on, Nico," I replied. "Anchovy has plenty in tank." And that's when the horse began its weave through the pack.

A glimmer rose in Nicolas's eyes, forming into a solid hope as By Jove Anchovy advanced. "Holy shit!" he said. "Do we get money if it comes in third?"

I ignored him, giving all mental focus to the race. "Come on, By Jove," I said as if voicing my encouragement transmitted extra pep to the horse's gallop. Then I encouraged louder. By Jove was slick, it moved to third, and there was room for more.

"Let's go, Anchovy!" yelled Nicolas, who rose to his feet with a fist in the air, raising the intensity. The other gamblers turned and gave Nicolas the eye. I stood, too, By Jove Anchovy was making a last bolt, neck and neck with the leader, a big chestnut named Newtonian. Nicolas and I called our horse home, louder with each cheer of GO! GO! GO!, jumping in unison with the horse's strides.

By Jove Anchovy won, by a head.

Nicolas and I hugged with hoots of victory. Then Nicolas started crying, looking upwards to the cracked, textured ceiling, thanking his grandfather. By Jove Anchovy wasn't the favorite nor long shot, but the odds paid handsomely, and we collected over $300 each.

Nicolas wanted to gamble more, and I was tempted to let him so he could learn about gambling comprehensively. But I was in no mood to watch over such a lesson, and it would have been a buzzkill. I grabbed Nicolas by the arm and pulled him close. "Yes, this is great fortune," I said quietly, making sure he maintained eye contact. "The trick with good fortune is to enjoy it. Look around. Do any of these men look like they're enjoying fortune?"

It was a sight. Pot bellies, heavy sweats and blotchy faces. "You're right," Nicolas said, letting the rush subside, coming to his senses. "I just won 300 bucks."

"And that gets plenty of fun." I picked up the pitcher of beer, then motioned to the doors that led to the grandstand. "Come on, let's check out the rest of the track."

We wandered around the enclosed grandstand that looked outdated in a Soviet way. It was grey and dusty, the benches defeated, private booths with black and white mini televisions, the old kinds that were cube shaped. I wanted to check the view from the Members Club, but it was boarded up.

The stables were weeded over, no oats or hay or any sign of horse. Then we made it to the track. The dirt had been removed, leaving the asphalt base exposed.

"The best thing would be a foot race," I said. "The final 300 yards, down the straight, to the finish line. It will sober you some. This is a good way to honor the decades of thoroughbreds who have raced before us."

Nicolas liked the idea, and he started to stretch. Then he asked, "Do you want a head start? Maybe 10 yards?"

"What the fuck?"

"I don't mean to be disrespectful. I just work out five days a week. You said a race, right?"

His tact was stupid, but I could understand his view. I was older than Holly and Holly was nearly ten years older than him. And it had been a long time since I had actually run, probably the last time I rode a bus since I had a habit of being late and always running to catch it. That was over 5 years ago. Still, I never missed a bus. I was an exceptional runner in my youth, and although those days were in the Kurt Cobain era, I have the mentality of a runner, it has never gone. At any given moment I believe I can leap and outrun anything.

"That means first past the post gets twenty bucks from the loser," I said.

I let him lead for the first hundred yards. The enormity of the final stretch, out front, tasting the air before everything else with the grandstand looking on—I wanted my young out-of-town guest to feel the thrill.

The next hundred yards I narrowed the gap but remained a step or two behind, doing so silently. Like whispering death. He looked ridiculous, running in rolled up jeans and tucked-in striped shirt. Like a sailor in pajamas.

With a hundred yards to go, I went Mad Max, the valves in my heart opened wide, the lungs heaved deeper, my strides like pistons. We were neck and neck, but for some reason I couldn't take the lead. I searched deep for speed, inhaling and exhaling loudly, and when I pushed the pace a little more Nicolas matched it. We crossed the line side by side, but I kept running, my teeth clenched, trying to grind every bit of energy out of me. Then I started to laugh, but it didn't sound right, it was an unfamiliar pitch, and I realized it was Nicolas who is laughing, and he's still running, too, right there beside me. ⬣

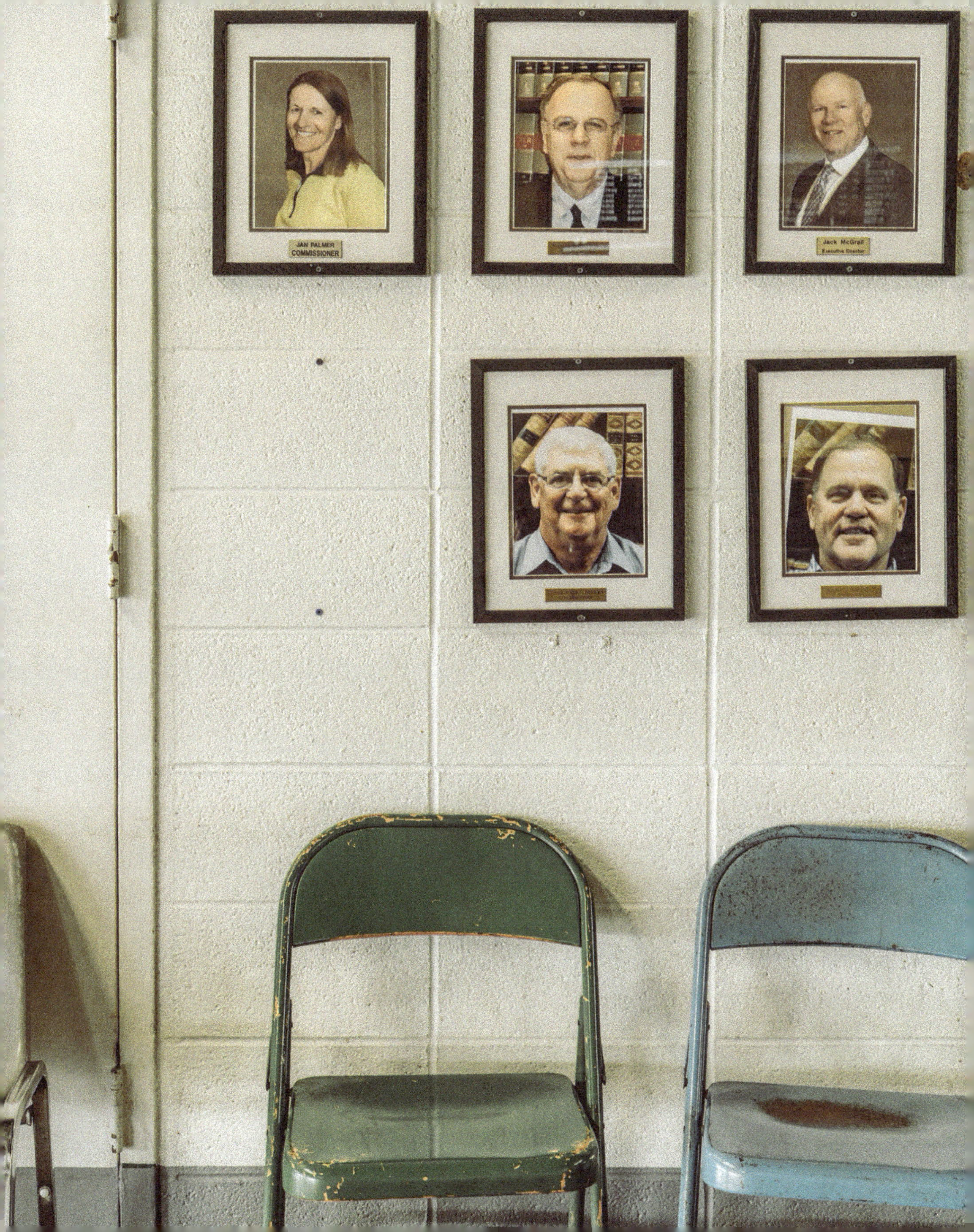

JAN PALMER
COMMISSIONER
Jack McGrail
Executive Director

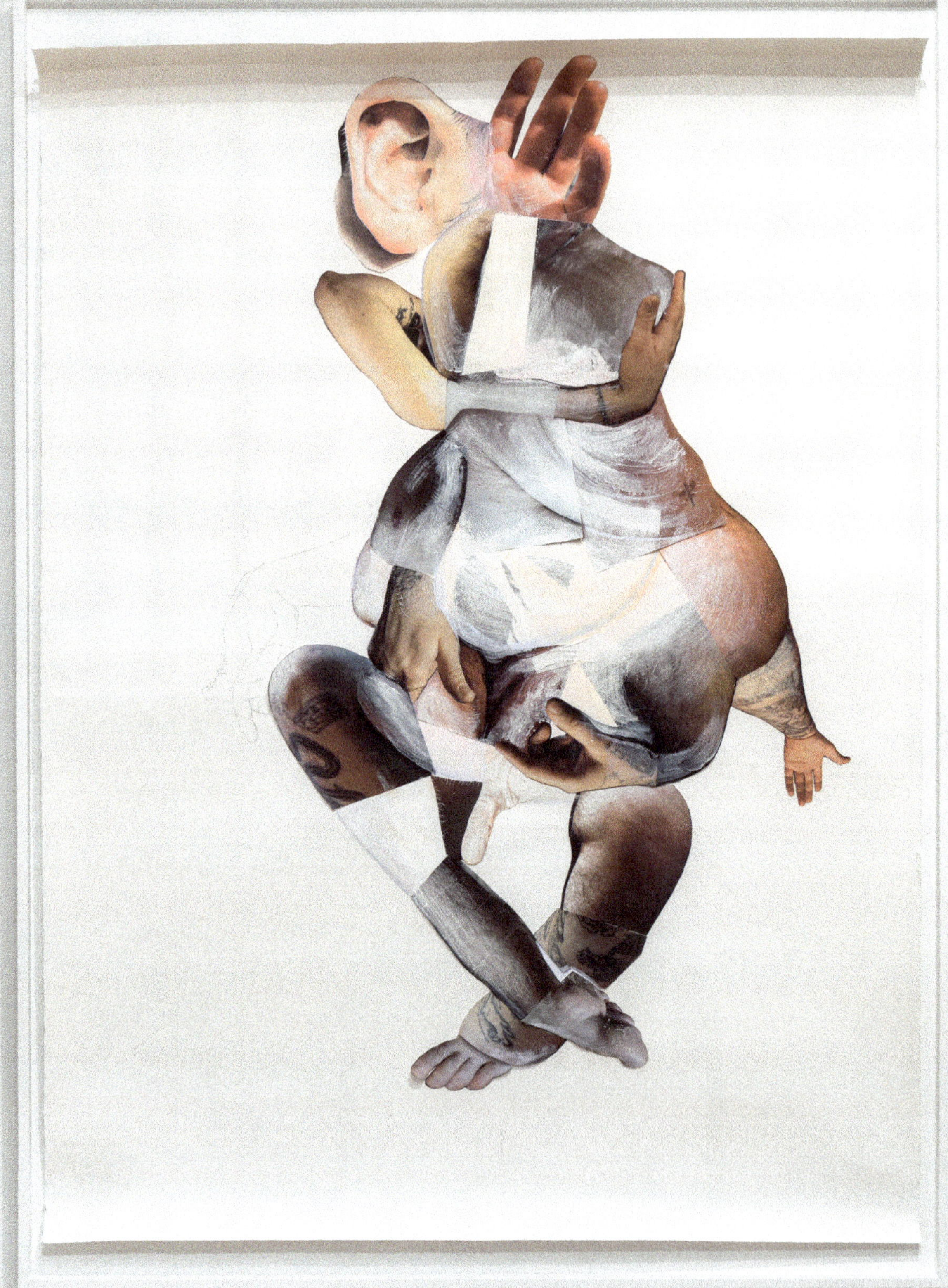

TORSO WALL

Words by Joe Galván
Artwork by Allynn Carpenter

Joe Galván was born and raised in Harlingen, Texas. He has been writing all of his life. His work has appeared in *Texas Monthly, The Believer, Harbinger, Barrelhouse,* and *Deep Overstock*. He received a certificate in Prose from the Independent Publishing Resource Center in 2019 for his collection of short stories, *Sereno,* which draws from his Catholic faith, Latin heritage, and love of the Baroque. His influences include Georges Bernanos, Fernando del Paso, Toni Morrison, Joan Didion, Elena Poniatówska, Jorge Amado, John Cage and Jacobus de Voragine. You can visit him at http://tilde.town/~joe.

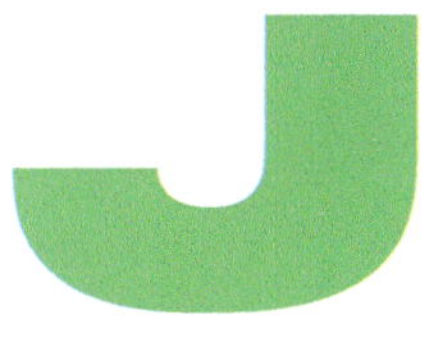

ustin Chu's iPhone pulsed like an artery, delivering the quicksilver blood of meaningless drivel that coursed through the world on mere currents of electric air, from satellite to satellite, access point to access point, through his jeans pocket and into his brain.

The same twenty-eight year old he'd seen the other night with the six pack aggressively proffered up a clandestine tryst in the shadows of the Red Lion, insinuating, cajoling, conjuring up images of a room with light-blocking scarlet curtains where no one would see the inevitable and a tiled bathroom where the douching and apologies would take place. It was all too tempting on the evening commute.

He called himself Rich.

'No one would know you'd be here,' Rich said. The first thing that Justin noticed when he tapped on Rich's profile was the way his ab muscles rippled into the tight v-shape before the pubic hair curled upwards around his belly button. An athletic type, like they all were now,

Chinese bots or not, another anonymous torso on the Torso Wall on Grindr, a catalogue of pectorals and deltoids glistening under the cold white fluorescent lights of many anonymous gym bathrooms.

'I just can't,' Justin typed back. A vagrant with bare smelly feet sat next to him on the MAX and he held in his breath to avoid inhaling the yeasty smell. 'I have dinner with my parents at seven.'

The MAX bell rang and the car pulled forward into a blur of faces and trees, stoplights and crosswalks. For six days now the same account messaged him from a glassy tower defiantly rising like a fat crystal phallus. The GPS sensor gave an approximate number of steps to meet Rich in his hotel room or his midcentury loft with his bondage gear and his harnesses and his video head cleaner and his jockstraps, accoutrements of lust and oblivion. Justin hesitated always: to meet or not to meet?

The dumpy-looking women clutched their purses, and turned away in their seats to avoid looking at the vagrant, who stared blankly into the distance. Justin could feel the hair on the back of his neck raise. Just as he put his phone away, it buzzed against the top of his thigh. Another message.

'Come and meet me for drinks, then. I'm in the lobby downstairs.'

'Lobby where?'

'The lobby of the Quartz Building.'

The crystal dick has a name, Justin thought to himself.

The MAX reached its next stop and belched out a crowd of tired people. Justin stepped out and saw the pink-glassed shard standing out against the purple sky.

He passed the Red Lion and walked down the hill. He crossed the street and a nervous twinge inched up his back like a caterpillar. What if Rich was a catfish? A fat guy? A criminal?

The building was a lot more chaotic up close: its lines veered off into the sky at strange angles, bulbous pendant lamps made of bamboo hung like rotten fruit from the naked concrete ceilings. Justin stepped in and heard the sound of a fountain gushing water from a minimalist niche in the concrete. No one was in the lobby except for a figure standing before the plate glass windows in the sunlight, watching the river sparkle.

'Rich,' Justin said.

The man turned around. He was shorter than what he said he was: 5'9, maybe 170 pounds, and it looked like he worked out a lot. Justin's heart pounded.

'Oh hey, you found me.'

The words fumbled out of Justin's mouth.

'I had—couldn't—well, I found you, yes. Yes, I found you. Hi. I'm Justin.'

Justin put out his hand Rich pumped it.

'Did you have anything in mind? Like, did you want to get tacos or something?' Rich asked.

'I thought—I thought you said you wanted to—'

Rich nodded. 'Well *yes*, I thought we'd get something to eat later.'

Justin looked at his phone. Six-thirty-six and

FOR SIX DAYS NOW THE SAME ACCOUNT MESSAGED HIM FROM A GLASSY TOWER DEFIANTLY RISING LIKE A FAT CRYSTAL PHALLUS.

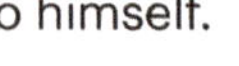

all around them the evening traffic hummed.

'Sure, if you know a place around here.'

'We could just Grubhub it if you want,' Rich said. 'I don't mind going back upstairs. Or we could get coffee.'

'No, tacos seem fine. Do you—would you mind telling me where the nearest bathroom is?'

'In my place,' Rich replied.

The entire apartment looked sterile, functional, anodyne. Rich said he lived alone and it showed—scattered gym clothes on the hardwood floors, a pantry devoid of food. On the naked countertops lay house keys and sneaker boxes.

'What do you do, Rich?' Justin said, washing his hands.

'I work in tech. Government bids. Construction.'

'Oh really.'

'Yes, really,' Rich replied. 'You?'

'I just do front desk for a state agency. Nothing special.'

Justin turned around and Rich was leaning on the doorframe, arms crossed, looking at him.

'I'm not rich like you are,' Justin said. 'This is the nicest place I've ever seen.'

Rich looked at him like he had heard the compliment before.

'I'm not wealthy. Just lucky.'

'Lucky how?'

'Are we gonna get tacos or not?'

'I'm not naïve,' Justin said. 'I know you were just wanting sex when we first started talking.'

'I was wanting sex. But you're cute and I wanted to get to know you too.'

'I thought you were going to hate the way I looked.'

'You look fine.'

Justin raised his shirt and showed Rich a roll of baby fat just above the waist of his jeans.

'This is *disgusting*; I'll never have what you have.'

'What I have,' Rich said, 'is good genetics. I can eat garbage and never gain a pound. It wasn't always easy though. I don't really get the time to go to the gym. Work takes me all different places.'

'That's completely surprising given where you live.'

'I'm a country boy, born and raised. From Bend.'

'I thought you had a boyfriend. When I saw your profile, I mean. I thought, "This guy is taken and just wants a third." '

'I did have a boyfriend. I was going to marry him, even,' Rich said. 'Relationships don't work out the way they're supposed to, I guess. Before I moved out to downtown I was living in Gresham with my folks. Didn't have a job or a car. Like I said, I was lucky. This more or less just fell into my lap.'

'I wish I had your luck,' Justin said. 'I front desk because I'm unhireable.'

'Why's that?'

Justin shrugged. 'I went to PSU, got a good GPA. My major isn't all that interesting, so I didn't jump on a job like everyone else did after graduation. I just drifted. I was... wanting to leave home, maybe live in San Francisco.'

'And then what?'

'Well, nothing,' Justin replied. 'Nothing happened. The bottom fell out. I'm stuck here.'

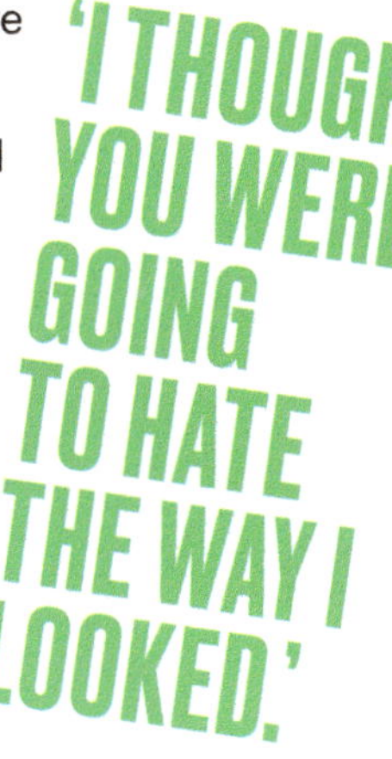

They downed a last shot of tequila together and headed onto the terrace. The liquor dulled the anxiety Justin had about being held by a stranger, albeit a handsome one. They kissed. He felt Rich's stubble brace his neck, tasted his warm breath tinged with the bitter notes of tequila and lime. All around them the city bustled ceaselessly; the traffic whizzed past the Burnside Bridge into the heart of Old Town, time

the screen wakened.

'It's four-thirty. Oh fuck,' Justin replied. 'I gotta get home.'

He rolled out of the bed and nearly slipped on the polished wooden floors.

'What's going on?' Rich said.

'I gotta work today. At eight AM.'

'Where do you live?'

'Tigard. Like, SW 170th.'

THE BOTTOM FELL OUT.
I'M STUCK HERE.

arrested in the humid night. Rich took his hand and led him back toward the bed. He pulled off Justin's shirt and tossed it to the ground.

Before long Rich was on top of him, pulling off his underwear and straddling his abdomen, ripping the packaging off a condom with his teeth. Justin ran a hand up Rich's abs and nudged his chin.

'Quit it,' Rich said.

'I can't help myself,' Justin whispered. 'You're too cute.'

'Fuck outta here with that,' Rich said. 'No one has ever called me cute except for my last ex-girlfriend.'

Rich linked a leg together and jiggled Justin's paunch.

'Don't touch me there,' Justin giggled. 'I'm too fat for you.'

Justin awoke, freed himself from Rich's embrace, rolled over and checked his iPhone. His pupils contracted in a blur of bright light as

'I can give you a ride if you want.'

'You'd do that for me?'

'Sure. It's not a problem. We should get some breakfast first, though.'

He peppered Rich's deltoid with a few kisses.

'I'm sorry,' he said. 'I'm sorry I lost my erection at the beginning. It'd be a little bit better if I had... you know—just relaxed...We didn't even climax together.'

'You're a good kisser,' Rich replied, not opening his eyes.

'Is that all I am?'

'No,' Rich said. 'I don't meet dudes who kiss the way you do. I used to not like it at all.'

Justin blushed. 'My ex used to say that.'

'What was he like?'

'An asshole, a lawyer. He went to Lewis and Clark and all that. A total bottom, of course.'

Rich nodded and rubbed the sleep out of his eyes.

'So, do you wanna take a shower? I reckon I gotta be up, too.'

Justin nodded and they went into the shower together.

For a moment Justin felt like he was in middle school again, demurely soaping up his ass in a tiled shower filled with strangers who bullied him. Rich watched him get naked and turn the hot water on. They got in together and Rich's libido awakened; in the silver mist Justin felt another part of Rich unfold itself into him, like a vine creeping toward a staff to choke out its life. Rich put his tongue in Justin's mouth. It took less than twenty minutes for Justin and Rich to top each other, and Rich was done, he left Justin to gawk at how old he looked in the floor-to-ceiling mirror.

After they both dressed, Rich walked Justin, work bag and all, down the stairs to the parking garage.

'It's still early,' Justin said. 'A good start on traffic isn't a bad idea.'

'Let's get some, I don't know, waffles or something.'

'Waffles? You can do that with that body?'

'Bruh. I fuckin' love to eat. Especially after sex or before the gym.'

'I hear you,' Justin replied. 'So…was that a good date?'

'I HEAR YOU,' JUSTIN REPLIED. 'SO…WAS THAT A GOOD DATE?'

Rich shrugged. 'I guess. I mean, it's a hookup, right?'

'A hookup,' Justin replied. 'That's right. I guess you don't wanna hang out then after this.'

'I never said that,' Rich replied.

The only place that was open was the breakfast joint on Powell that all the club kids went to on Sunday morning, a cramped, busy restaurant that smelled of grease and still had very old walnut panelling. On this morning, though, the restaurant was dead, with a few truckers, some crustpunks flipping through a copy of *Pork* and a few hipster girls reading tarot.

Rich ordered a black coffee and an omelet plate, and very carefully made a hot pink little pool of Tabasco to dip his eggs in.

'So, you never told me what you are.'

'Excuse me?'

'I mean what race you are.'

'My parents are from China. Guangdong to be exact.'

'I didn't check,' Rich replied. 'I guess it doesn't matter. I mean I'm not on Grindr all that much.'

'I have to ask then,' Justin said, sipping his orange juice, 'Why did you ask me to come over? Why me specifically?'

'It's been a long time. I usually don't mess around much with Asian guys. It was a lucky break.'

'Oh, I get it,' Justin replied. 'No fats, no femmes, no spice, no rice? You white guys really are all the same.'

'I'm not racist,' Rich replied. 'I just haven't had a lot of experience.'

'I'm confused,' Justin said. 'I already feel out of your league. I thought you said you had a boyfriend.'

'I did,' Rich said. 'He was terrible. And anyway. I'm usually so busy I never do any of this dating shit to begin with.'

Justin stared at Rich as he struggled to express this last salient point.

'Where I work… the guys I work with… you

know. I know Portland's an open place. But still. It's not like I'm in the closet. I long for companionship just as much as you do. To have someone to spend time with.'

'I'm still not convinced,' Justin said.

'You looked like a nice person. Like someone I could hold at night and feel comfortable talking to. I never get that. Never. Not at home, not at work. I can't even tell you how much I wanted to just hold someone.'

Justin let him have his confession, let it linger under the greasy table lamps amid the din of girls directly behind them chattering about the King of Swords. The traffic was picking up on Powell and quick. Rush hour had come.

'Either way it doesn't matter,' Rich said. 'I got what I wanted. I wanted to see you. I wanted to see you naked. I wanted to hold hands with you. That was nice. I never get that.'

They sat in Rich's pickup for about twenty minutes afterward and made out like teenagers. Rich's hands went up under Justin's polo until he could stroke the few chest hairs Justin had.

'I was thinking, if you wanted to do this again,' Justin whispered. 'We could.'

'I'd be open to it,' Rich replied. 'If you want to, that is.'

'You still OK with dating an Asian guy like me?'

Rich nodded, chuckling a little, hovering over his lips.

After they were done, Rich drove Justin to Tigard in the blue hour. He turned on the country music station and hummed a song he didn't know the words to, let Justin put his hand on his thick thigh. Justin smiled and looked on.

Justin saw the familiar outline of the building he worked in appear down the street. He felt a tug of sadness overcome him.

'What have you got going on for today?' Justin asked.

'I have to work, like I told you,' Rich replied.

The pickup truck pulled into the concrete cul-de-sac where the low squat office building sat. Justin pulled his backpack up from the floor of the passenger seat and clenched his jacket close to him.

'I'll text you?' he said.

'Yeah, sure,' Rich replied. 'You have a good day today, you hear?'

Justin kissed him gently and lingered on his lips.

'Thanks for taking me to work this morning.'

Justin slid his ass off the seat and pushed himself out of the truck. Standing on the concrete he was at eye level with the fat bulge of Rich's stuffed pocket, from which he could see the iPhone that had brought them both together.

'I don't know what you see you in me.'

'You shouldn't be so hard on yourself. I'll let you know when I'm free,' Rich said, smirking slightly. In the morning light, his blond stubble and grey eyes looked familiar, comforting, tender. Justin wanted to stay and look at Rich, masc as ever, his tricep bulging from the grey jersey shirt as he gripped the steering wheel.

He spent the rest of the morning at the front desk looking for Rich's Facebook profile. He wanted to know his last name and tried to remember clues about where Rich worked—which specific construction company he worked for, what his position was, how high up he was on the chain of command. He pulled up Grindr and stared at Rich's body, imagining himself close to it again. He took a screenshot and saved the photo to his phone.

When lunchtime came he sent Rich a message.

'I can't stop thinking about you,' he typed. 'I had a really good time with you last night. Miss cuddling you.'

'You're sweet,' Rich typed back.

'Can I see you on Thursday night?'

'Can I get back to you on that? I might have a party that night. If I can bring you along, we can go together.'

'OK.'

Justin sank back into his chair and closed his eyes, sighed, savored the relief of Rich's quick response. He was there, he hadn't just faded away into the yellow and black abyss of the Grindr hellworld. He sent Rich an above-angle picture of himself in the break room.

'I hope you're having a good afternoon,' he typed.

Thursday evening came and went. Justin sent two more texts before sliding into bed that night. He stared up at the ceiling and imagined Rich descending from the white spackle in a halo as blue as God's eye, resplendent and erotic. He imagined Rich's body meeting his in bed, entwining himself in the dingy white sheets he changed twice a month, kissing him in the way he'd seen people kiss in movies and on TV.

When Friday morning came his parents called him and asked to come to dinner. Justin, however, continued as if his fantasy never broke. He lavishly overspent at Starbucks and at a teriyaki place around the corner from work, imagining Rich would break on his lunch to see him. He ignored his parent's telephone call a second time. Justin knew Rich had seen his messages—every single one— and felt a frisson of panic. He hadn't responded. Saturday and Sunday were the same. Justin spent both days nervously stroking his cat and looking out of the window of his apartment, waiting to see if Rich might somehow guess where he lived.

Justin could see Rich's building gleaming in the afternoon sunlight. There was something so venal about Rich, achingly unreal and hypothetical, that even conjuring him up in thought was a dangerous act. If Rich was real—if his sentiments were real—they were nothing like what Justin could have ever expected from a hookup. But Rich remained elusive; as mysterious as the wall of muscled men on Grindr Justin wanted to be a part of deep down. Something felt unsettled, unresolved; indeed, something felt wrong.

On Sunday evening, he returned to a gym he hadn't seen in two weeks and did a half-assed leg set.

He got naked in the gym shower and took a solitary selfie. Justin swallowed back the shame and anger that he felt about seeing himself naked in the mirror in favor of what Rich might say.

'LOL,' Rich typed back. 'Is that u?'

'I've been wanting to talk to you all weekend,' Justin responded. 'I was hoping you'd like a photo of me naked.'

About two minutes passed, the chat bubble wavering, the dots jiggling in their digital bubble. Finally they disappeared altogether.

Justin put the phone down. He put his clothes on and took the MAX back home.

As the train pulled out of the second-to-the-last station his phone buzzed in his mesh shorts.

'Can you come over tonight?' Rich asked.

'Sure. I'm almost home.'

'I just wanted to say hi. Talk for a few.' Justin jumped to his feet, pushed past a few people on the MAX, and rushed out of the door. He started running past folks amassed on the platform until he felt the air rushing through him, until his feet had a mind of their own. The great glass phallus that stood against the starless dark was an immense and immutable Colossus that threatened to overwhelm him.

'I'm here,' he typed.

He paced back and forth under an awkwardly placed awning that dripped the dew of the night onto the smooth concrete walkway. A faint sour breeze cooled the sweat on his brow.

Rich walked out of the two glass doors. He wore a pair of mesh basketball shorts and flip flops, and for a moment Justin didn't recognize him. The shredder tank that Rich wore, though, gave him away—it was the same one he wore the first night they hooked up.

'I was hoping it wouldn't come to this,' Rich sighed. His voice was low and sounded troubled.

'What's wrong?' Justin replied. 'I've been wanting to see you all week. I haven't been able to stop—'

'Well, now I'm asking you to. I'm asking you to stop thinking about me.'

'Why?'

Rich put his hands on his waist and sighed.

'I can't get into it here. Can we walk somewhere?'

'I knew it,' Justin said. 'You're just like the rest of them.'

'The rest of who?'

'Everyone on that fucking app.'

'Calm down,' Rich replied.

'I'm fine,' Justin said. 'I can go if you want. I get it. We can't see each other anymore. I get it. I'm too fucking fat for you.'

'It's not *that*,' Rich replied. 'Jesus Christ.'

'Then what *is* it?'

Rich heaved a heavy sigh. 'Are you sure you want to know?'

Justin nodded.

Rich fumbled in his right pocket and pulled out a ring.

'I can't see you anymore. I'm married. To a woman. I was hoping you'd forget about me.'

'But you said you wanted to hang out with me. You said you missed me.'

'I did,' Rich said. 'I *did* miss you. I don't get those feelings a lot. With you it was different. But you can't text me like you have been. It's weird and confusing.'

Justin let out an incredulous chuckle. He took two steps back and turned to walk away.

'Justin! Come back!' Rich said. 'At least let me take you home, please.'

Justin ignored him. The sound of the overpass

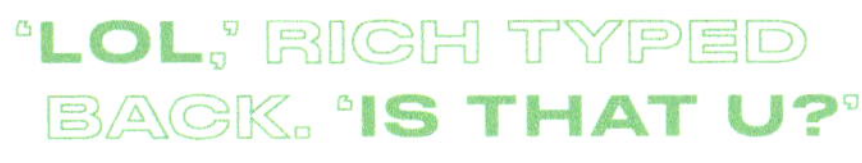

eventually drowned out Rich's voice. At the stoplight, Justin pushed the button, heard the buzz of the crosswalk, and kept walking. He walked as far as the MAX station and then two blocks further, until he was sure Rich wouldn't be able to find him. The pain from overtraining flared in his calves and he struggled to keep pace.

The same vagrant from the MAX toddled his way up the platform, barefoot and disheveled, and smelling worse than he did before. He pushed past a woman on a motorized scooter and nearly fell over her purple cane. He asked every single person on the platform if they had any money. The hair on the back of Justin's neck rose and he clenched his phone and wallet in his pocket.

The vagrant walked up to him and said, 'Excuse me, do you happen to have a dollar? I haven't eaten.'

'Fuck off,' Justin said, coolly. 'I don't have any money.'

The vagrant shook his head and moved on to the next person.

The MAX arrived, shaking and rattling on the iron bones of the tracks, its bell clanging in the dim, wet darkness. Justin felt his phone buzz two more times. He ran through the drizzle until he reached the end of the platform. He took the very last seat in the very last car. A pang of shame and fear pounded inside of him.

HE TOOK THE VERY LAST SEAT IN THE VERY LAST CAR. A PANG OF SHAME AND FEAR POUNDED INSIDE OF HIM.

The bell rang and the car pulled forward. Justin took out his phone and began to type away, the bright blue haze of the phone lighting up the tracks of tears that fell from his face.

The car pulled away. By the time Rich had arrived at the platform, the MAX had lengthened into the distance, until it was a solitary point of light that faded away into mirage of the wispy dark amid the patter of raindrops falling on the lindens. ⓑ

how I felt about it
to know
it took a long time

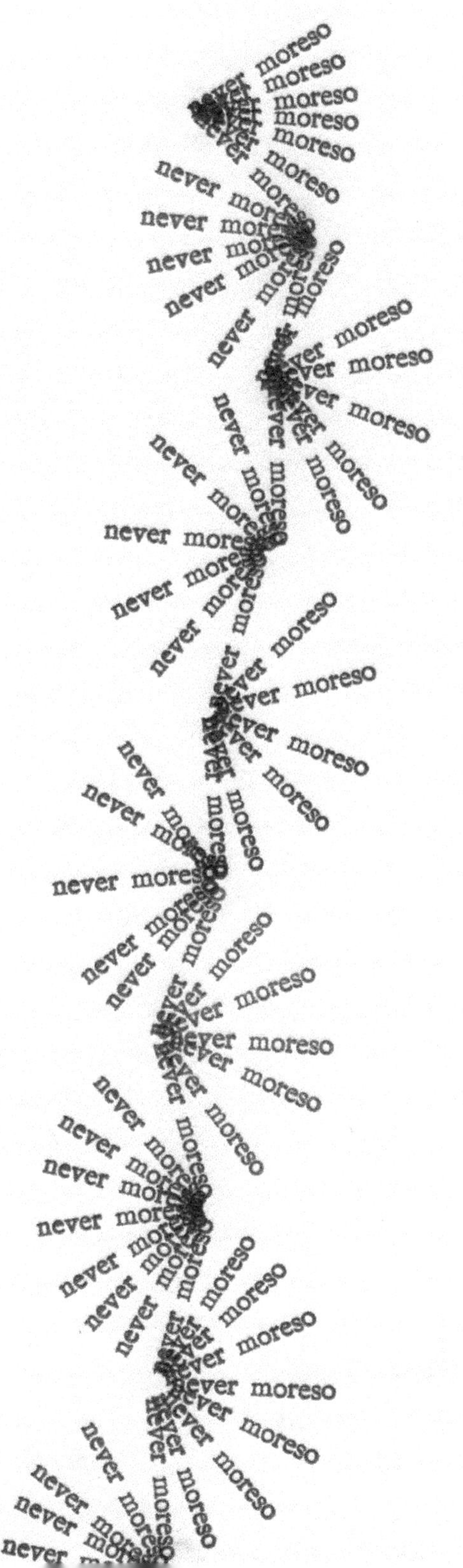

never moreso

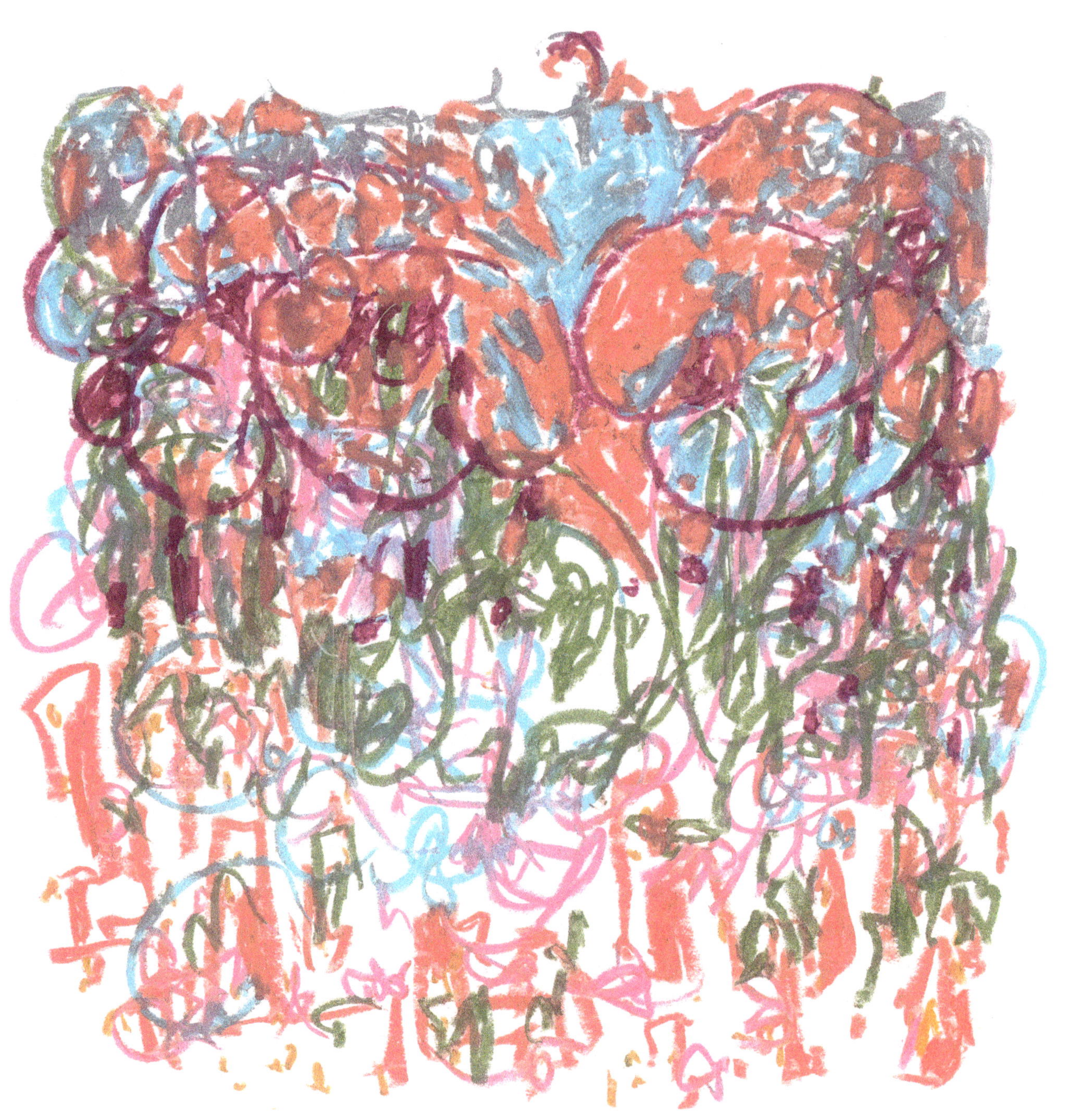

STRINGS AND SEALING WAX

Words by Arlo Voorhees

Artwork by Zachary Schomburg

A former farm kid and Fulbright Scholar, Arlo Voorhees sells cars in Portland, Oregon. Ya'll can find his poems, essays and translations in new issues of *The Moth*, *Muse/A, Confrontation, DIAGRAM, Rattle, Panel, Portland Monthly* and *1859*. "Strings and Sealing Wax" is a chapter from his un-contracted, rant/memoir: *Plugging Out: How to Preserve your Soul in Times Absurd.*

In the milk crate, tucked under a wicker who-knows-what that held our VHS collection, my Dad's records collected dust until at eight years old I seized upon them like a culture-starved Philistine. I was a farm kid on a dirt road in the hinterlands of nowhere. Those LPs were my MTV, my ticket stubs, my bus fare to the fabled metropolis of Worcester, MA. While my Dad's tractor groaned through the manure pit, I'd splay out on the thrift-store rug and listen, listen, listen. I had to be peeled from the cotton filaments to feed the calves, clean the heifer shed or whatever silly task my folks thought more important than developing an ear for music. Still, the notes stayed with me as I mixed Milk Replacer for the newly weaned or stacked hay forever on summer afternoons. Yes, I'd hum Dr. Hook's "Penicillin Penny" as the unloader dropped 70-pound bales from the attic of the hay mount.

Having finished my chores, I'd immediately put on a record and return to that rug. I'd listen both to the music and how my brain responded to every lyric. Yes, the burgeoning critic in me immediately started to shape good from bad. I'd devour the album art and ask questions. *Hey Robert Palmer, is that Sally in the background, and why exactly did you have to sneak Sally through the alley?* I'd flip those records again and again trying to make connections, and when I tired of the music detective charade, I'd just recline into the arms of a perfectly rendered folk song.

Though I discovered hundreds more in the attic at age 18, for most of my childhood I had about 15 records and tapes. I memorized every song on every album, even the ones that the eight-year-old me already knew were just awful. I mean really Moody Blues, did anybody actually buy your self-indulgent cliché-ridden nonsense? Some of the songs persist today while others have faded to the frayed edges of memory. Numbers like Bob Dylan's "Leopard Skin Pill Box Hat" sustained me in times of great depression, and others played in the background as I stumbled through the infancy of love. They propelled me through my adolescence because I knew them so well. These songs were best friends, first lovers, cross-country road trips, even soundtracks for psilocybin-sponsored field trips to that other dimension.

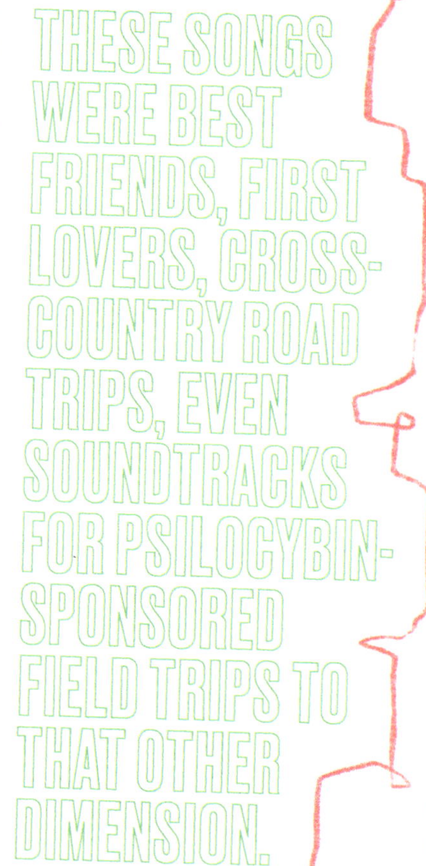

Ah, but that was then. Today, that eight-year-old kid and his parents don't have it so easy. We've changed the way music comes to us, and unfortunately, it doesn't invite intense deliberation. Most homes no longer have an electronic device that only plays music. So, what's the big deal? Everybody listens to music, especially young'uns. Those awesome goth kids are still discovering The Cure, and music continues to chaperone teenage misanthropes through the black waters of Lethe.

Roughly nine out of ten folks I know have a Spotify account. The remaining 10% probably use Pandora. These are our modern-day record players and they give us access to thousands of albums. A quick browse through the database can reveal that record you'd forgotten or, based on their intuitive algorithm, you might discover an altogether new band that will blow your mind out of your mind.

Yet the problem— which seems crazy, especially since every teenager since 1991 has spent at least half the day with her headphones on, is that our new musical devices and platforms actually discourage listening. But the digital music epiphany isn't all that easy. The internet has swallowed your radio just to spit it back up with all the other crap it's acquired throughout the day. Just as this typewriter is both enriching and destroying every sentence I type, the computer, smartphone and internet changes the music we listen to. When we use Spotify, we have eight different tabs open; we're composing emails to old flames, shopping for chic boots on Ebay, scrolling through Facebook or reading every factoid (which alas, we'll forget tomorrow) about the band in question. There's no space for that eight-year-old kid. No room for deeply absorbing every hallowed riff. A Spotify listener might not even notice when Bill Morrissey – at the end of the folk masterpiece, "These Cold Fingers-" is forced to shoot his dog.

And just like modern art, the music is transformed so it lacks social charge and has pathetically little soul charge as well. The less we focus on something, the more peripheral it becomes. No longer will we sympathize with the shouts from the fringes of civilization. Less exposed to the terror and sadness of our song-makers, we'll be less willing to explore these ideas ourselves—you know, those emotional ones that makes us unique, vulnerable and original humans. Even when we buy music online, we don't get to scour the lyrics like I did in 1988. We don't get to hold the lyric sheet and album art in our hands. Nor spill K-mart Cola or pilfered whiskey on it. We don't doggedly rewind to hear that verse again— the one you know unlocks the mystery of the album and its art.

I can hear your objections from here. Some of you use Spotify at home when you're sitting on the couch and doing fuck all but listening to music. If so, that's great. But is your phone really stowed somewhere you can't touch it? And are you listening to something you actually want to listen to? Because you're so adorable, let's say you're one of the noble ones; you've recently purchased a digital album and are presently ransacking the lyrics and the album art on your tablet. It's entirely possible, but circumstances suggest otherwise. I totally just re-tweeted a picture of the singer looking forlorn against

a graffitied brick wall, and Oh look, that KISS t-shirt you wanted is still there, and the online auction is ending soon!

In short, these music platforms make us less dynamic, more suited for the status quo, more likely to mistake pastiche for art and capitalism for counterculture. Or, to really put the hay where the goat can get at it, music gets worse as does our appetite for raw, brilliant, complex emotion. In super short, we get as dumb and one-dimensional as the music we've miraculously ignored though we surround ourselves with it. Music becomes just another tab on an overloaded browser—something you might revisit but by the time you do, another song has already started, and do you really have the patience to look away from your screen, close your eyes and actually listen, listen, listen.

Let's take an interlude to Eastern Europe in the 1920's. In *Raggle Taggle*, Irish scholar and musician, Walter Starkie, recounts his days traveling through Hungary in Romania with nothing but a fiddle. It was the 1920s, a time of

TODAY, WALTER STARKIE WOULD BE SHOT. 100 YEARS AGO, HE WAS LET IN.

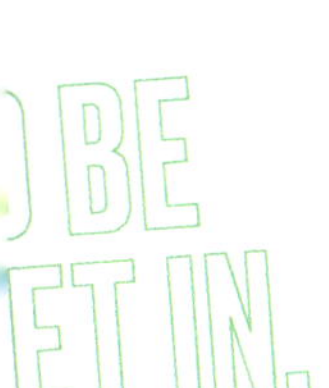
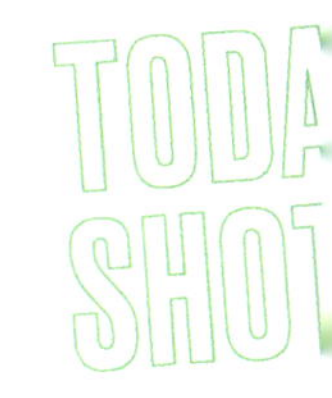

extreme misfortune and post WWI confusion, especially in Hungary, who had just been stripped of 57% of her land. Prosperity was far out of reach. A disheveled peasant class had little to share and a lot to complain about. Nevertheless, how did Starkie acquire lodging as he headed east across the Great Hungarian plain? He played music. Regularly, he posted up in front of a thatched-roof house and plays a folk song on the fiddle.

Think of it. You live in the middle of nowhere. Everything you own is your livelihood. You wouldn't let bandits drive away your livestock nor strangers rummage through your shed and take the few useful tools you had left. You had to be vigilant! But suddenly a haggard stranger emerges from the bushes and starts playing some goddamn music.

Today, Walter Starkie would be shot. 100 years ago, he was let in. Not out of sympathy or that fabled Hungarian hospitality. It was purely for the sake of the song. Music was a gift. These folks didn't have radios; maybe they heard music once a year at a harvest celebration, and it was always live. You didn't get to pick when you heard music. Such was the power of a lone fiddle. Come in and have the last of my soup and stay as long as you like.

100 years before that, John Keats writes "Ode to a Nightingale," a beautiful, desperate collision of lack and nostalgia. He hears the nightingale's song and so desperate is he for music and haunted by the depth of its song, he feverishly composes a poem in rhymed nuanced iambic pentameter in a futile attempt to imitate the nightingale. Only a man, he fails,

for he is consciously orchestrating his verse and cannot, whatever he does, mimic the pure spontaneity of the bird's aubade. Just the same, Keats' poems persist because he tried to make that music—such is the power of euphony. Such was the power of song.

Such is the power of nostalgia that beckons me back to those records. Days spent cleaning the maternity pen and singing Harry Chapin songs as if it was my duty alone to keep those songs alive.

Nevertheless, this argument is not just reminiscence. Nostalgia resolves itself in the past because the days of yore were simple and therefore more authentic than the grotesque and terrifying present. My childhood, and the late 80's and early 90's, was anything but simple. I simply want us to temper our acceptance of all things new, to remember ourselves in the rush to upgrade. I want us to remain content when working with minimal content. I want you to lay on the floor with a glass of whiskey and listen exclusively for music. ⓑ

MISSED CONNECTIONS #12: HANDSOME YOUNG VEGETABLE MAN

Words by Joel Preston Smith

Artwork by Brianna Spencer

We sort of met and didn't meet at Safeway. You were groping the avocados. I said something about how the two of you should just get a room. You looked around like somebody was there (only no one was there) and then you made a funny face. Are you an actor? Commercials? I know I've seen you somewhere. You're really really good. I regret not asking for your number. Even more I regret you didn't ask mine. ⓑ

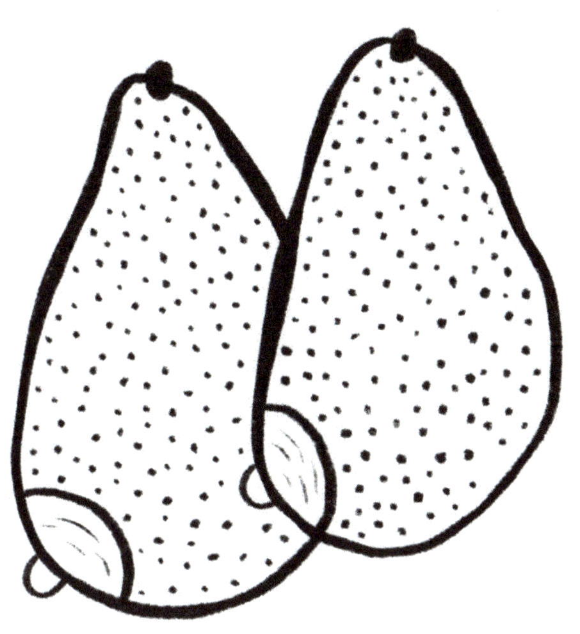

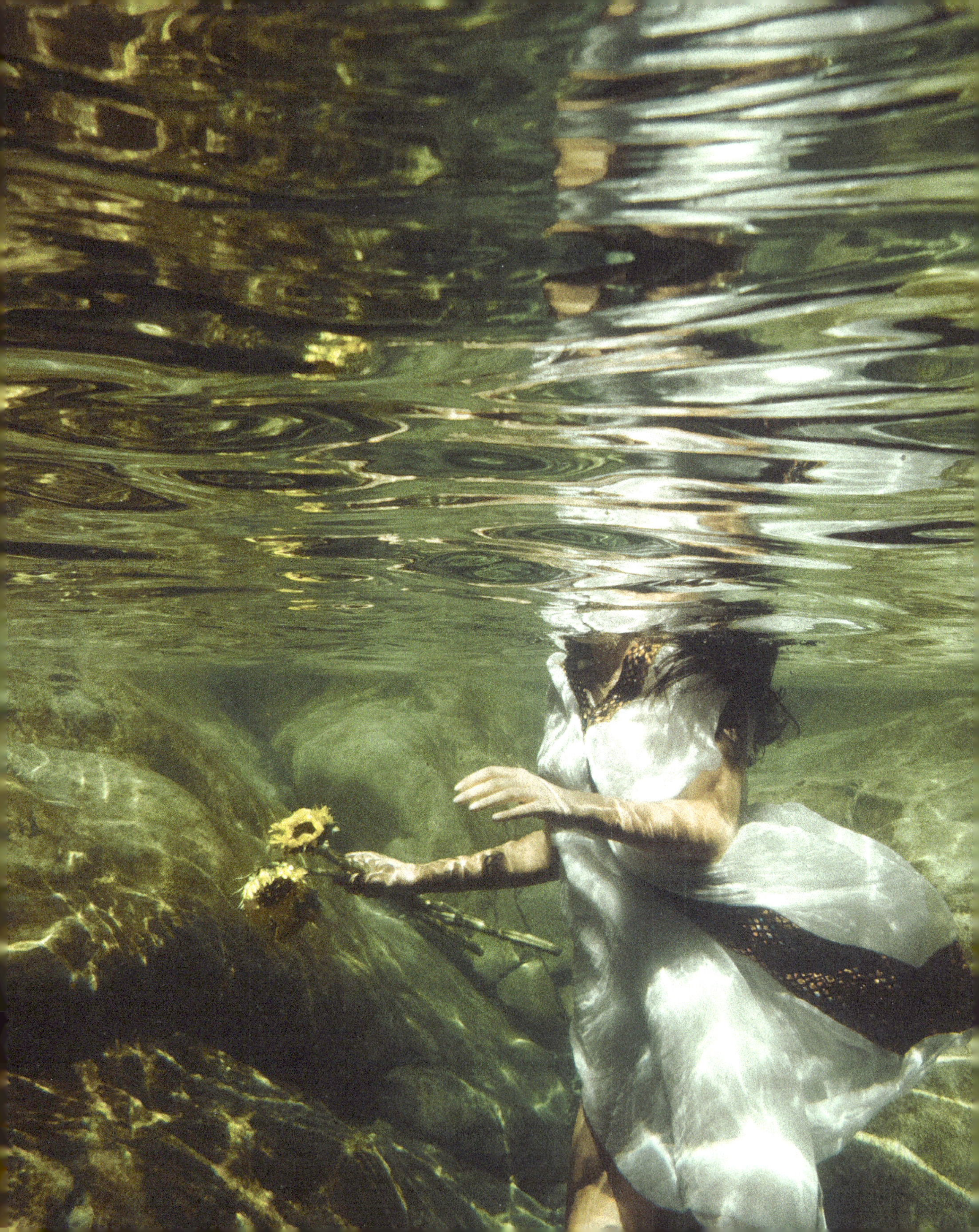

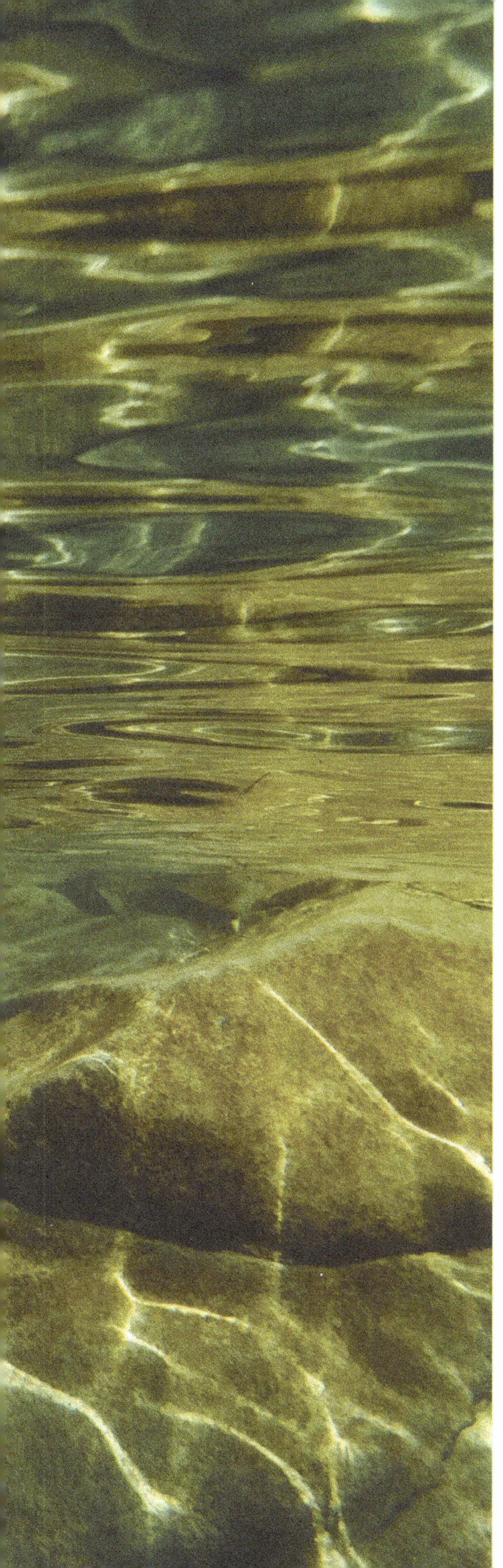

RACING JOSEPHINE

Words by Tammy Stoner
Artwork by Amanda Jackson

Tammy Lynne Stoner is the author of the award winning, southern novel, *SUGAR LAND*, publisher of *Gertrude* literary journal, and wrangler of the GERTIE queer book club. She spends half her life in the bathtub and the other half in flannel pajamas. TammyLynneStoner.com

- *Igloo*

I sleep inside an igloo in my efficiency apartment across from the Jack in the Box on Pine. An igloo I built out of carefully stacked empty fifths of whiskey, one row upside down on another, so that the bottlenecks interlock. To secure them in place, I weaved pieces of red and blue fabric between the two rows like grout.

I'm alive, I think every morning when I wake up, because every night in my dreams I'm dead. Killed by my mother, my preacher, or myself. It's hard to believe I'm alive when so many better people are dead, but each morning my eyes open to a ray of sunlight shattering across the bottles all around me. It feels like a glass dragon has swallowed me whole.

I do a few skin pinches with hands as cold

as a nun's anger to confirm the life I feel, then I push up and crawl out of my igloo to face the world—or the harsh light of the fridge, or maybe the Handy Man. He pops in here to check on things. I think my daughter must've asked him to watch out for me. She must have told him that I'm a drunk and a danger to myself and others.

The Handy Man asked me to call him Hank. When we met he asked me why I didn't have any furniture. Why I was living down here. Pretty thing like myself. I just smiled back.

Hank is five feet nothing, with a wide head. I think he's only two-dimensional, but I don't have proof of that. I once asked him if he turned sideways, could he slide through the crack on the edge of the door.

"I'll fix that," he said, completely missing my point.

+++++

I'm forty-five. My daughter is twenty. I married her father. Maybe that was a mistake but you do what you gotta when you need cash. Besides, if you overlooked the warts on his hands, he was almost handsome. And I loved him—in the beginning, before he became what I always told him he would. No sense hoping an entire gender can suddenly redeem itself with the gentleness of one man. Besides, they're only gentle so you relax and don't bruise as easily later.

+++++

When my daughter was 13, I snorted quite a few lines over the sound of the toilet flushing. I did that many so I could be strong enough to let her in on my secret. Make her part of my world. I was really trying to give us something to share, some secret spot before she ran away—because I knew she'd run away someday.

I came out of the bathroom, running my finger over my gums, and started right in. I told her about *The System* I'd discovered—the mode of transportation that takes me around my brain on a tour bus, walls flashing scenes that I can step into.

I said, "It's because time doesn't move in a straight line, honey. Time zigzags all over the place and I'm not sure if it does that just in my head or if it does that in everyone's world but either way it's real to me, understand?

"Time travel requires an *altered state*," I continued. "I've gotten it down to a science. If I want to stay here, I drink beer. If I want to go to happy spots in my past, I drink Chambord. If I want to feel love, I drink wine. If I want to go check out the angry spots, I drink whiskey. If I want to go into my future, I drink rum or Jagermeister. Anything with syrups. Sugars speed you up. See?"

When I looked over, her flecked blue eyes were cloudy. The same way they all turn eventually, some just take longer than others.

+++++

I sweep and clean the bathrooms down at Johnny's Joint five blocks away. He pays me with a twenty and free shots. Cheap, white label well shots, but I don't much mind. I minimize the swill-booze-morning by drinking a glass of water at bedtime followed by a glass of caffeine-free Pepsi and two aspirins. Then I shovel down a few crackers and pass out. In the morning I eat two or three spoonfuls of spicy beans and cheese from the fridge with a can of beer.

+++++

I had a stroke two years ago. Before that, I'd been throwing up and had diarrhea for about six months—gastritis. They had to shove tubes up my rectum three times before that man down at the clinic correctly diagnosed me.

The gastritis didn't go away until they put me on antibiotics. But when the pills ran out the shits came right back, angrier than ever. Luckily I clean bathrooms for a living, so the toilets are always close by.

After a few months of this, the doctor said my electrolytes had depleted themselves. This screwed up my potassium. That's when I had a stroke—a mild one. They watched my heart for a few days then sent me home, telling me I couldn't drink more than one glass of water a day or my system would shock itself and my old ticker would tock.

Two weeks of that bullshit and I was up to speed again, back working at Johnny's. Those two weeks were rough—luckily I'd had pills to cut the edges. I did a lot of time travel then, thinking about my daughter. I remember how proud she was the first time she learned to wave; how scared I was when she fell off her bike, a bruise the size of a plum on her forehead. I remember the picture she drew of me in third grade with a big purple head and spaghetti-hair. I wasn't smiling. I worried back then—worried about her and me and us. Every second of every hour I worried, even when I slept. My brain felt like it had a second hand on it that just spun and spun, making all kinds of barely audible noise— the sound of worry.

When I was pregnant, I prayed for a boy because I knew the world was cruel to girls, but that doesn't mean I didn't want my little girl. It just meant I stopped smiling and I started worrying.

+++++

91

Johnny owns Johnny's Joint. His hair is as tall and greasy as a strip club cock. His real name is Milton. Milton Havordford. He builds the thing piled on his head by applying black dye shampoo, then mousse, then hairspray. No conditioner. To maintain the height of his swirl, he sprays his hair while hanging his head upside down.

He combs black dye into his chest hairs too. Maybe one time he had a nice chest, before everything sagged. Now he's tanned to a crisp orange, like well-roasted duck.

Johnny pees in front of me. Says he likes to be the first in the bowl every day, mark his

Johnny tells the bar (again) that he's never fathered a child. He had an accident in Vietnam that left him infertile. Not impotent, just infertile.

"Every man should be left infertile after their tour of duty. Just set it up like a metal detector that the men walk through before they step on the plane home," he said. "We'll all think they're checking for weapons but what they're really doin' is leavin' you with blanks."

"Fine idea," Sick Bob says.

I think Johnny's bulimic. Come morning, there's always a few flakes of vomit under the toilet rim.

territory. Makes a big show of pulling out his cock, holding it loosely, spraying slowly. When he shakes off, he pulls a little more than he has to. Tells me they should make a "puller" with the urinals. A hole that sits above the bowl so a guy can straddle the porcelain and pop his stiffy in for a good tug. Says he always feels like getting his rocks off when his bladder's full.

"If they ever invent that machine," I say to him, "*I quit.*"

Johnny laughs, zips up, and leaves the graffiti and flickering light of the bathroom. There are five people in the bar, mostly men who drive at night. Sick Bob, who sometimes barbacks for free drinks, calls out: "Joh-nay!"

"Sick Bob!"

They call Sick Bob sick on account of his runny nose. Once I saw Bob sneeze into his hands and then lick it up, that's how sick he really is.

Johnny's always hinting about his weight— wondering if a certain pair of jeans looks too tight or if he should wear stripes or if white's too much for him. He is a little on the round side, at least from the ribs down, but his legs and arms are skinny enough. I once told him that if he ever has the baby he'd drop a good forty pounds. He told me he didn't need me to clean that day—that I should go home before I miss my afternoon shows.

But then the next day he gave me Makers Mark shots instead of well, and he asked what my favorite 45 was so he could load it in the jukebox.

"I was a little hot under the collar yesterday," he said, smiling, his eyes resting like tired birds on my breastline. They're good, my breasts—but it's not without help. The only thing I really spend money on are bras—well, bras and mascara, since the shitty stuff clumps.

"My favorite song is 'Strange Fruit,'" I told him. "Billie Holiday."

Billie and me, we bite our own asses. We both want someone to watch over us, but when we find them, we tear them to pieces hunting for the bad parts. This makes our lovers become what we fear, but we don't care. What matters sometimes is who's first out of the gates.

I've found that if you tear into something enough, you'll turn it bad. Every time. It's the lucky ones who die before the tearing breaks them open, shaking out a tiny, solid seed of black evil. We've all got the seed. Better to die than to see the seed fall out and take root. I'd rip open every vein I had and drink down every drop in Johnny's if I knew for sure I could kill the seed and not me.

Sometimes I dream that Billie and I are howling like alley bitches in heat after all the men have gone home. Howlin' out all the old songs. Crying. Passing a fifth of gin between us. Smoking menthols with lipstick smudges around the filters. She asks me if her flower's on straight.

When I wake up I know these aren't dreams. I really *am* singing with her. There's some religion that believes our entire existence is just the dream of a god. If that's true, then who's to say that our dreams aren't really happening somewhere else?

A good hunk of my dreams seem to be old reruns of shows I didn't much care for the first time around. Someday maybe I'll get the strength to re-write the endings. My daughter says I'll never do any re-writing if I'm always boozing it up.

My daughter is the main reason I don't get a phone again. That way I won't have to listen to myself slur out "I Love Yous" with a puffy tongue. Holding down the mute button while I pop another beer tab. Forgetting the stereo's on so of course she knows when it's muted.

- Boneyard

Her father (my husband) and I made up after I quit Johnny's last year. Three months later he sold the last of our dope, took the car, and houdini'ed. He left all his shoes and socks behind, walked out in his slippers with a backpack full of T-shirts.

I stared into the empty dresser drawer, then gathered up all the credit cards in his name and bought a bottle of Chambord, a used pickup truck, and enough food to fuel me on my drive to wherever I would end up. I also bought my daughter a bottle of Chanel No. 5.

On the seat next to me sat my daughter's old doll. Something I take with me no matter where I go.

I drove for three days, listening to Tanya Tucker and scratching my itchy feet on the gas pedal until I came across a sign hanging at a roadside diner just outside Olympia, Washington. The sign advertised free rent in "a dome" in trade for help working the gardens. I dropped some silver into the phone and gave a call.

Domes—geodesic domes—are prefabricated houses held together with leftover hippie hope. They hump onto the earth like ladybugs, with skylights for black dots on their backs.

The gardener, who placed the ad and who owns the dome, calls himself Smithy. He adds the -y to his name because he thinks it sounds friendly. He tells me I was the only one who answered the ad, so I got the job as his assistant.

"My flowers," he says, "are renowned for their longevity and height. It's all about my special fertilizer—coffee grounds and moss biscuits. Family secret." *Until now*, I think.

Smithy looks like what I think a gardener should look like—tall, thin, bearded, wearing overalls, sunburned nose. There's a sweetness to him that makes me feel like everything's going to be OK. That there's no sense getting upset about anything.

Smithy's lady—Theresa—used to be a man. When she was going through the conversion, she had to wear a huge plastic penis inside her surgically constructed vaginal cavity for months in order to stretch it into shape. She can't have an orgasm vaginally, so she prefers anal sex. At least that's what she told me one afternoon when we shared a pitcher of vodka and lemonade.

I looked her up and down. "I'd never have known you used to be a man."

"I never was," she said. "Not really."

Theresa paid for most of the hormones dancing at a club in Portland, Oregon. Dancing made me think of my beautiful daughter, which made me think of having more lemonade. So I did. Theresa, meanwhile, went on talking.

"Smithy is the only man who's ever loved me as a woman. Maybe the only man who ever loved me period, except my father. My father is amazing. When I told him I was switching teams, he just said, 'Well, I hope this means your cooking will improve.'"

Come Christmas time, Theresa and Smithy gave me a guitar—an old nylon string, no-name acoustic with a handful of neon green picks. For some reason they thought I'd always wanted to learn the guitar. Must've forgotten telling them that.

That was months ago. Now the furniture's splintering, my nails are permanently lined with

MAYBE THE ONLY MAN WHO EVER LOVED ME PERIOD, EXCEPT MY FATHER. MY FATHER IS AMAZING.

dirt, and the outdoor insects have decided they prefer it indoors. And Smithy and Theresa's niceness is starting to wrap around me like intestines.

The only way out is to find a man, maybe even one with a job. I could set myself up in a SRO downtown, maybe do another cleaning gig—only this time I'll follow the proprietor's lead when he pulls it out. Maybe.

I still got looks enough to inspire. Maybe.

Or *better*, I'll get a job in a nursery. Tell them what I know now about flowers and mulch and rotation and watering before the sun comes up and yellow leaves brown leaves broken leaves bitten leaves droopy leaves white-dotted leaves. Talk the talk. I could meet a nice man there, buying flowers for his mother or his secretary or his dead wife's grave. The wife he thought he'd never replace.

I'll dry out. I'll doll up.

Thinking about it, I nearly knock myself over laughing. Thinking I could stand to stay in one place for the rest of my days—ha! Thinking I could stare into the sun without a shield—ha! Thinking I could leave Billie all alone in her alley, me waving goodbye with my three-piece-suit-man coiling himself around me. Ha!

Who cares about the world, we'd shout two hours later. *Who cares!* You're beautiful. I feel so comfortable around—oops—around you.

Then they don't come back because they don't want to feel *that* comfortable around anyone. They want to impress you with their three-piece suits and bleached smiles, their laidback smarts, and their tight asses.

The man who delivered the package had eyes that looked like my little girl's eyes before she understood. Like glass polished to a shiny ice blue by a kitten's tongue.

+++++

THINKING I COULD STAND TO STAY IN ONE PLACE FOR THE REST OF MY DAYS—HA!

+++++

Met a guy yesterday. He came by to deliver a package to the wrong address. He said I looked like Shirley MacClaine. I wanted to say that I didn't know who Shirley MacClaine was—that I don't get out much. I wanted to say, Stay with me. I wanted to say that there's a spot inside me that won't stop crying and there's another one that won't stop laughing and I'm not sure which is sane so I just sit in between the two. But all I said was thanks.

Besides, I'd tried it before. I'd invited them in only to say one stupid thing after another to fill the space between us. There's nothing worse than watching yourself say one stupid thing after another before figuring it'll be easier, flow better, be more comfortable with some amber on rocks. Maybe they'll relax, too.

Would you like a drink? *Sure!* Then: Another sounds great!

It's time to move along, I told Theresa and Smithy. You've been great to me but I need my own space. I've decided to dry out and fix up and stand tall and walk strong and shake firm and talk quiet and think clear and re-write my endings.

Theresa cried, her Tammy Fayes running down her tan cheeks.

I clipped on my sunglasses, hopped in my truck loaded down with my guitar and some quilts they made me keep, put Billie on the stereo, and took off. I drove and drove, past patches of grains and razor-sharp mountains. Air so smooth you didn't know you were breathing.

+++++

Somewhere in the middle of California I drove by an overgrown cemetery that seemed strange, familiar. I stopped. I felt like reading the stones and smoking.

"Stretch my legs," I said to my daughter's

doll, buckled in on the passenger's side.

The day was cool but something inside me blew hot. I walked through the boneyard's ankle-high grasses as if I was being led by someone. I walked on and on in a strange daze.

Near the end of the third row, I bent over one of the smaller, overgrown headstones to light a match, and read the name: *Josephine Marit.* Josephine, my beautiful little girl. My daughter who, according to the chiseled dents, died six years ago—23 days before she turned 14. She fell off a pier and drowned. She wasn't twenty—no, she was 14 plus 6 years dead.

And just like that my heart stopped beating. My skin turned cold. Time shifted again: Officers were asking me if I knew she couldn't swim. Of course I knew, I answered. *Of course I knew.*

- Desert

The next thing I know, I am racing out of the boneyard and flying down the freeway toward Palm Springs, as fast as I can. My guts churn and my head looks for a time spin.

Palm Springs. I figure the desert might be as good a place as any for a lady such as myself to find refuge. I drive fast with all the windows down and the winds grow hotter and hotter until it feels like I'm trapped in an oven. The air down here doesn't blow, it wobbles. I push the gas pedal down further and sing on the top of my lungs to kill my thoughts.

+++++

The A/C in my truck only runs cold when it's cold outside—when it can pull in cold air and take credit for the work. The heater works, though. Maybe I should have turned north—too late now. I drink Chambord and vodka from my travel mug. My mind races.

In the bright sunlight, I see my daughter in her fringed bathing suit—a one-piece, though she'd wanted a bikini—on the pier. Her Daddy drove off the day before. I toast her and I yell out that she shouldn't jump in, but she does anyway. I lean back and close my eyes in the peace and quiet.

I call out to her from my lawn chair—thinking she's playing with me, but she never surfaces. I run over, screaming the whole way to the pier. I jump in past the sludge along the edge and don't feel a thing except this vice strangling around my throat.

I gag from all the water splashing up as I struggle to find her. My eyes aches and my arms are moving so fast, fueled by some unseen energy force.

I dive under over and over and over and

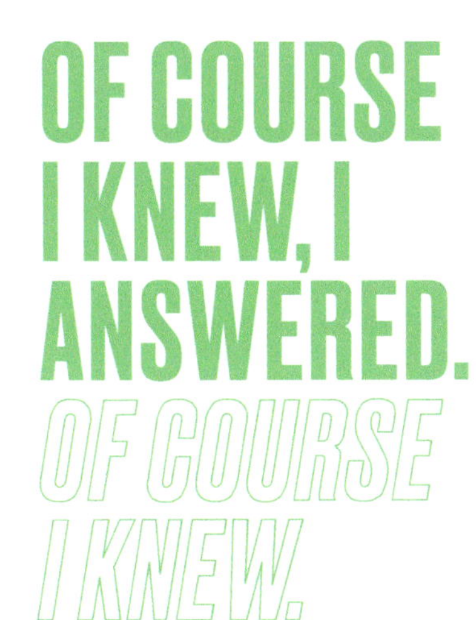

I WORRY ABOUT IT EVAPORATING IN THIS GODDAMN HEAT, EVAPORATING BEFORE I CAN GIVE IT TO HER.

over again until there she is—her foot lodged between two slick rocks. I pull and pull on her body under the water, not caring if I yank her foot clean off, as long as my baby is alive. But she's not. She's limp and heavy and gone.

+++++

I still have Josephine's Chanel No. 5 in the glove compartment. I worry about it evaporating in this goddamn heat, evaporating before I can give it to her. That worry, plus a need to use the facilities, forces me into a bed-bug just off the freeway. A tan and tan single-story gig with, it seems, a pool and free HBO. It also has, I note, a cute little watering hole attached to it with a sign for a *Waitress Wanted* taped to the front door.

I push up my boobs and walk in. ◉

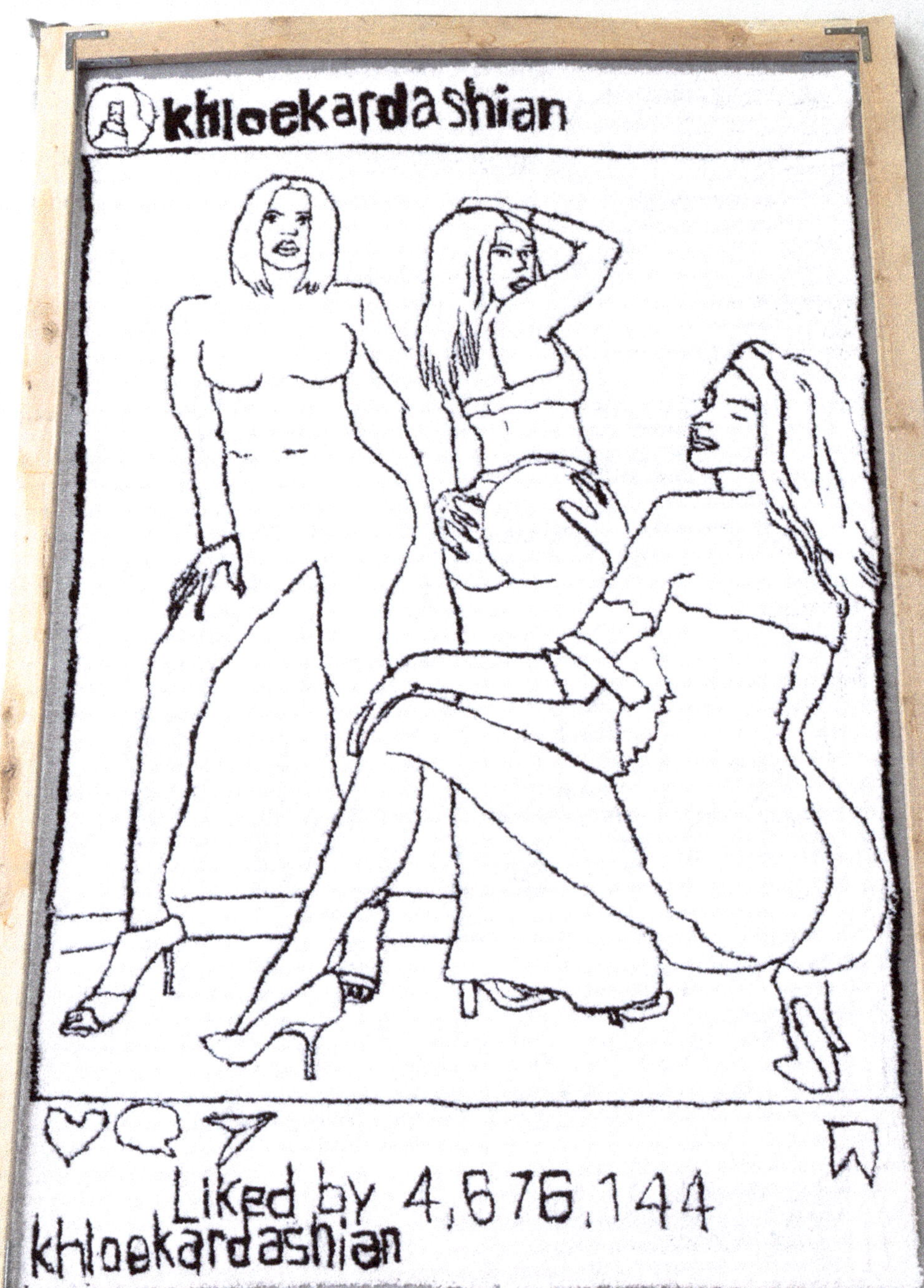

khloekardashian
Liked by 4,676,144
khloekardashian

LAUREN PRADO:
SCHEMES, THE AMERICAN DREAM, AND THE KARDASHIANS

Interview by Jess Andra
Artwork by Lauren Prado

Jess Andra is an artist, musician and writer living in Portland. At the time of this interview she was manager at One Grand Gallery, but has since stepped down.

Inquiries: jessandraxo@gmail.com

In August 2019, One Grand Gallery was pleased to show new work by Lauren Prado: *Schemes, the Kardashians, and the American Dream.* **We sat down with Lauren to hear about the motivations behind her work.**

Jess: In the past, you worked as a teacher in California, and recently you earned an MFA from PNCA. Could you tell us about the journey, and how you got to where you are today?

Lauren: I just finished grad school and that was fun, right? Two years of school. Before I came up here I was a high school teacher, and I taught at an iPad-only high school: no books allowed. It really showed me a different perspective on this millennial lifestyle.

The kids were always on their phones and always on their iPads, because that's all they had. In my classroom, it would be like 7:30 am, first bell, and these kids were waiting for a Supreme drop, you know, at 8. They had to be the first ones to buy it. They had everything they wanted in a cart, basically, and were waiting to check out as soon as it dropped. It was this whole other culture I had not been aware of. Seeing kids buy all these fashionable things, then turn around and sell them, or just keeping up with fast-paced trends, was super eye opening. It got me started down this line of research: **How much does social media have its grip on us—what we do, how we act, what we buy, and what we wear?** Because I was seeing that a lot in the kids, but also if we look out into the 'real world,' adults do it as well. So from that experience I kind of spiraled into looking at celebrities, and specifically the Kardashians. It inspired the work I did at PNCA.

J: So you went to grad school at PNCA... are you back to teaching again?

L: I just graduated in May, so I'm just chillin for now.

J: You've been working with sewing and textiles for a long time, how did you get into that?

L: In my undergrad, I start school like "I need to make money, I'm going to be a nurse." So I start taking all these bio classes and shit, and I fuckin' fail out. I'm all "fuck this!" Then I don't tell my parents, and I change my major to be an art major—what I really wanted to be in the first place. I take my first art class and my professor's this awesome hippy lady. She's like "Where've you *been*, kid?" and I'm like "Thank God. I finally figured it out." She was teaching this dye class, with critique and fabric dying and she's like "Take my class. You'll love it." So I jumped right in, and I fell in love. From there I started dying fabric, sewing, quilting, and that was the big

turning point for me. Of course I've always liked to sew, my grandma taught me how to sew. I would sew my own Barbie clothes and shit. But that class was really the turning point for me to do a full dive into this medium. It's progressed from dying and stuff like that, to sewing more and tufting now—making those rugs. It's been quite a journey.

J: Interesting! You went from dying fabrics, to sewing pictures of shoes, to tufting these rugs.

L: Yeah. At first, I was sewing the shoes on clear canvas. It's what grandmas use to cross stitch, basically. So I was using that grid to sew shoes.

From there, I started seeing all these videos on Instagram, of people using a tufting machine to make rugs.

I'm like "What *is* this?" So I dive into trying to find it. It has to be on Amazon... Syke, it's not on Amazon. It has to be somewhere. So I google all around and just find this one guy who sells them in the United States.

I bought it from him. The machines don't really come with instructions, it's a figure-it-out-yourself kinda deal. And that's what I did. I was winging it. It was also difficult to figure out, like, what type of yarn is compatible, or what fabric works the best. It was really trial and error for awhile. I think I finally have it down now.

J: Was the decision to make your rugs so big because of the size of the tufting machine, or was it more conceptual?

L: It was a little bit of both. I'm always a sucker for "go big or go home." Also with the Kardashians,

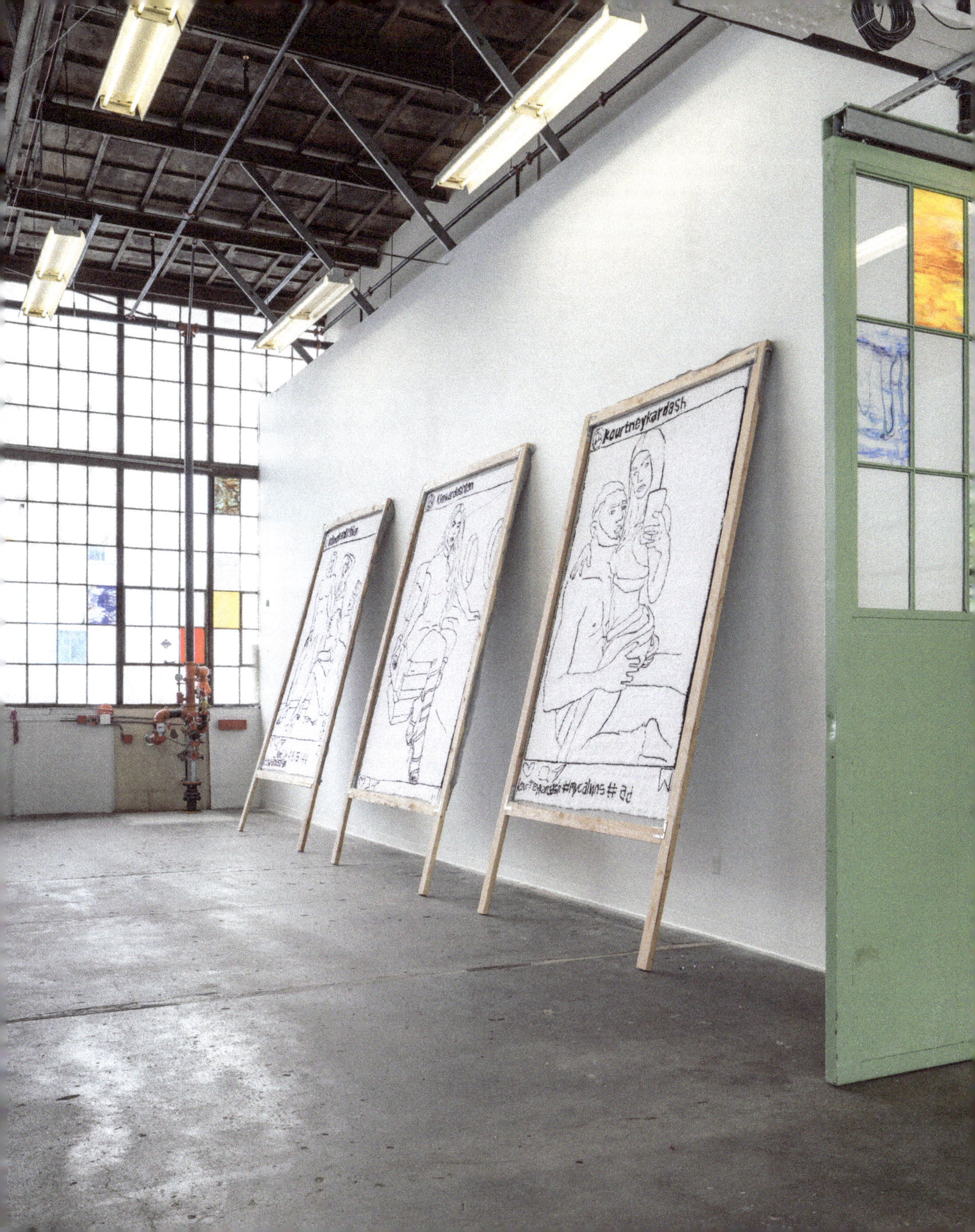
kourtneykardash
Kimkardashian
kourteykardash #mycalvins #ad

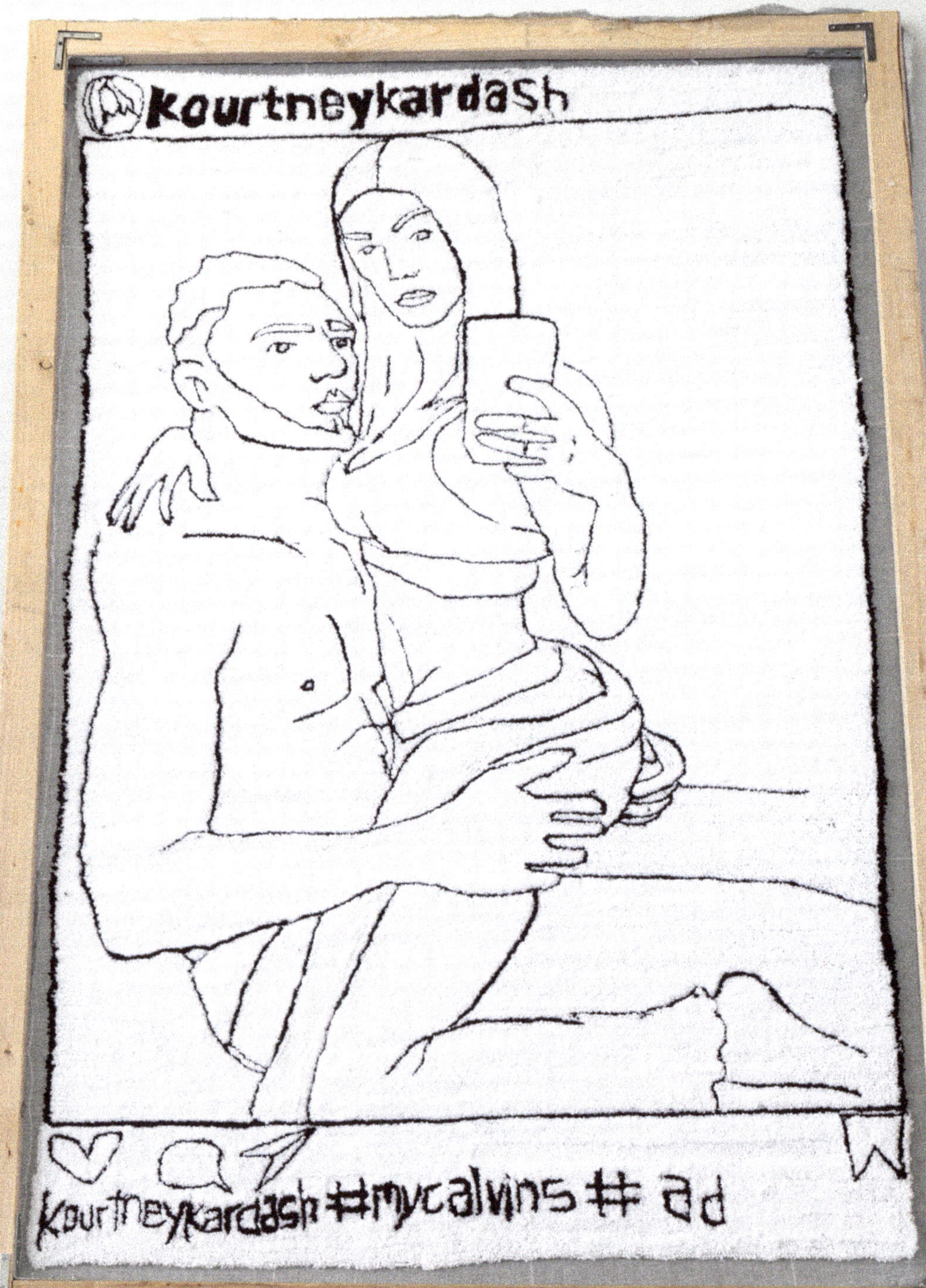

kourtneykardash
kourtneykardash #mycalvins # ad

I'm thinking about their range. They're, like, *insane* celebrities. I figured these would have to be bigger than your regular throw rug. That's the number one reason why they're 12 ft by 7 ft.

Also conceptually, thinking through the Kardashians, what they represent, and their connections to consumerism and the American dream. For me, the saying "go big or go home," runs parallel to the American dream. *Work hard and you'll get everything you want! or Why just shop for a few things? Shop for everything you want!* I saw a lot of parallels with both aspects.

Also, you know, using such a big tool and writing with it, doing details are more difficult when you're working smaller. But if you want to write KIM KARDASHIAN and you want it to be legible, it has to be a little bigger. So that's kind of another reason.

J: So the fact that they're rugs... how does that play into it?

L: I always think about this goal of ours as a society: *Reach out and grab it*, you know, *you CAN*. There's this weird tension where, the piece is an art object, set in a gallery, and you know the rules: Don't reach out. Don't touch... Yet there's something about this tactile quality of the rug where we're so accustomed to living with it and having it in the home, and we know what it probably feels like. **There's something about that weird tension where you want to reach out and touch it, but you can't.**

This medium really calls out to physical touch. I relate it to the way we interact with our mobile devices. You have to, like, double tap that heart on Kim's newest sexy selfie.

I think a lot about touch, and I think about this medium as a vehicle for desire, like you want to touch it. Just like when you go into the store and you want to touch a t-shirt before you buy it. Something is there. It's innate, and it's human, and I could go on forever about it. It's super weird that fabric has that much power over us.

I just always go back to desire, and there's something about making the Kardashians something that we touch digitally all the time into something soft, fleecy and sexy. It's like a sexy rug of someone who's sexy, who we already touch all the time digitally, it's full circle for me. It's just... the Kardashians, you know?

J: There's also the association of rugs being on the floor, and you're hanging them up, right?

L: Yeah, and I'm thinking about elevating. Rug you step on, rug you walk over, but these rugs... after you buy them, sure, do whatever you want. But the way they're displayed on the wall, there's a different connotation. We're elevating. Also the rugs, the big ones, are on frames. They have a little extra space at the bottom.

I relate that to celebrities and how we elevate, and put them on a pedestal. Once again thinking about the Kardashians, and this empire they're created for themselves, and how so many people look to them for so many different reasons.

J: What is the intended effect on the audience?

L: I'm obsessed with things that influence our culture, but I'm not trying to cast judgement at all. I am here to ask questions about celebrity and the American dream, and if this is all mimicry, you know, if we're just copying what we're seeing online. In turn corporations are monetizing us and our mimicry. **Is everything just mimicry? How deep does it get? Are we all basically being scammed by cliques and coolness online?** In the end, if a viewer can walk away with some of these questions, that will be

2019) so, like, you can't avoid it. If you can at least grasp the idea of these celebrities and how unavoidable they are, that's enough for me.

J: Where do you think this culture is going? What are your hopes and fears? What are you anticipating for the future?

L: I'm just paying attention to what's happening, and not really assuming or guessing where it's going to derail or whether its going to stay on track. Basically just pointing and writing what I see, like an anthropologist. I'm not trying to change everything. I wonder "Is it bad?" but the American dream has always been like this. The only thing that's changed is technology and how we access it. I don't see it stopping any time soon, and I don't really want it to, either! I would get bored.

IS EVERYTHING JUST MIMICRY? HOW DEEP DOES IT GET?

great. If someone wants to take the time to talk to me about it and hear a spiel about my idea behind it, they can.

If viewers walk away like "Damn that's a sick rug," I'm happy with that too. The viewer can come away with, at least, "That's a really big Kardashian rug."

If you go online, try as you might to avoid the Kardashians, you can't, I'm sorry. I believe the *New York Times* just wrote about them. You just can't avoid it. No matter what you're looking at, where you're trying to google, one of them is going to pop up. I think Kanye just got on the cover of Forbes magazine today (July 10,

J: So you usually like it, for the most part? Social media?

L: Yeah.

J: And are there lessons you've learned in the process of making this work?

L: Lots of people have been reaching out because they're seeing more tufting guns on the internet. They want to know "What gun are you using? What fabric are you using? What yarn are you using?" I try to help people as much as I can from the knowledge I've gained through trial and error.

But there's still a lot of stuff I don't even know, like trade secrets that other people on Instagram won't share. It's kind of crazy, you know? If you see someone doing the same thing as you, why not help them figure it out?

But people just won't share the information like "I got my fabric here, in bulk." People tell me to go to JoAnne's and get monks cloth, but actually that's not the best fabric to use. It's just hard because I can't find the real name or distributor for really large-scale fabric except for one chick on the internet and she upscales the stuff through the roof. I want to be like "Hey girl, just tell me the name. I'm going to buy it in bulk." So there are still obstacles to figure out, like for me, the best way to make these rugs without ending up broke. Anyone who reads this and has a suggestion can shoot me an email. Tell me what fabric you're using! I'm still trying to figure it out.

J: Do you feel your curiosity shifting at all? Do you have ideas for what you'd like to work on next?

L: At the moment, I'm still kind of super obsessed with the Kardashians and making the rugs. I'm going to branch out; I mean she posts a lot of pictures daily and all her sisters do. The three big rugs were of the three sisters: Kourtney, Kim and Khloé. Now I want to do Kendall, Kylie, and Kanye. I think people will really like that one. We'll see. I have some drawings, waiting to be turned into rugs. I'll stick with that for awhile.

J: Kanye seems like the perfect bridge between your previous work, where you were making sneakers, and this project.

L: The crazy thing is, Kanye is totally a bridge; but so is Kendall, and basically the way they all have contracts with these other companies is insane. That realization sparked my interest. I sewed the shoes, then other value objects like embroidered Lamborghinis and embroidered Ducati. Then I was seeing all the connections between these value objects and the Kardashians. Their matching G Wagons, and so on. I realized all these objects are important ties to one major family, the Kardashians. (The American dream). ⓑ

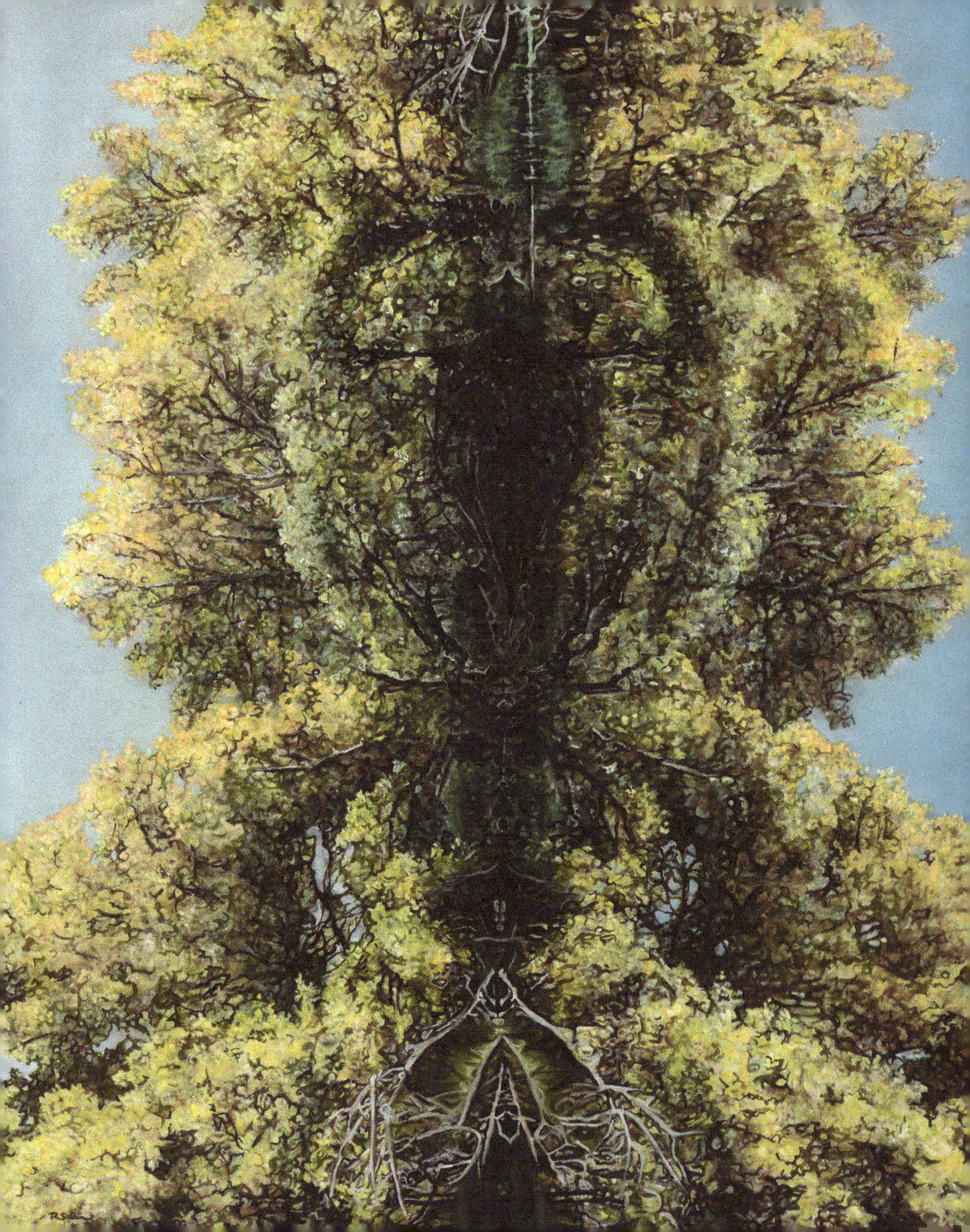

THE DEER MOTHER

Interview by Francesca G. Varela
Artwork by Rachel Sabin

Francesca G. Varela is the author of three novels: *Call of the Sun Child, Listen,* and *The Seas of Distant Stars,* which won the 2019 Independent Publisher Book Award for Science Fiction.

After growing up in West Linn, Oregon, Francesca received degrees in Environmental Studies and Creative Writing from the University of Oregon, and a Master's in Environmental Humanities from the University of Utah. She focuses her writing on environmental issues, and her forthcoming novel, *Blue Mar,* incorporates climate change, industrial agriculture, and plastic pollution as themes.

When not writing or reading, Francesca enjoys hiking, figure skating, playing piano, identifying wild birds, plants, and constellations, and traveling the world.

Paula couldn't remember when she'd started eating lunch at her desk. Slowly, gradually, over the last few months, she'd traded the conference tables by the microwave for her cubicle, more and more often, day by day, until, finally, she ate alone every afternoon.

She'd hoped no one would notice, but of course they did. One day, Alicia dropped by her desk and sat on the edge of it. She was a top-heavy woman in her mid-forties/early fifties who wore rhinestone tank tops beneath her blazers. Paula liked the tone of her voice—smooth like a yoga teacher's.

Paula used to sit with Alicia at lunch, along with a balding, gregarious woman named Sally, and a slim sixty-year-old named Phil who liked to tell Paula about his ten-mile runs.

"So when did you become an eat-lunch-at-your-desk person?" Alicia asked. Paula wasn't sure what to say. They were kind and inviting people, but lately she just hadn't *felt* like it. She was tired of their small-talk about reality shows, or their plans to go cycling on the coast that weekend. She needed to sit fallow. To stare at the computer screen and pretend she was typing reports.

"I've just been busy," Paula said. "Catching up on some things."

"Far more dedicated than the rest of us. You know, I was watching something on CNN about how millennials have a stronger sense of loyalty to their workplaces than any other generation."

"Oh, really?" Paula highly doubted that was true. She felt no loyalty to Bailey Insurance, and she only worked here because her mom's old friend once dated the recruiter, and he'd given her the job without even interviewing her. Maybe another year, and then she would be out of here with a healthy resume and paid-off student loans. And then? She had no idea. Sometimes she felt like she wasn't really grown up yet; like she was just a kid playing dress-up. High school, and college—they'd just happened, hadn't they? Just days ago, it seemed.

Phil paused at the opening of Paula's cubicle, a Mickey Mouse coffee cup in his hand. "You coming to lunch?" he asked.

"Oh, no. I've got some work to do."

"Don't we all." Phil laughed. He hesitated like he might say something else. For a moment Paula thought that they might try to convince her further, but they didn't.

Alicia patted her on the shoulder. "Don't forget to take a break now and again."

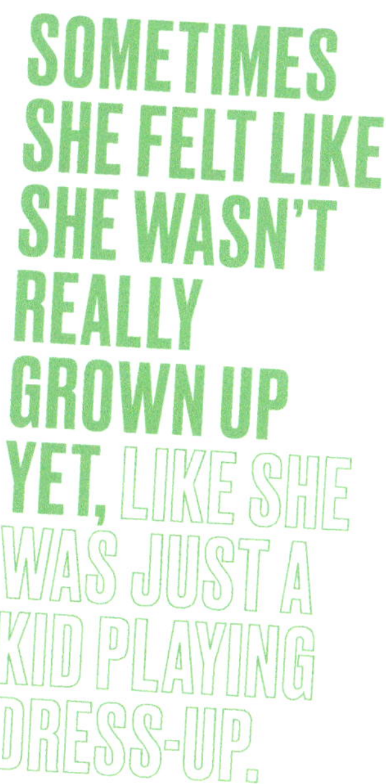

Paula thought about telling them she'd join them tomorrow, but that would have been a lie.

+++++

Ena put on her nametag. It was the faded green one from when the store first hired her. She hadn't changed it in all these years. It wasn't a pretty thing—part of the paint was chipping off in the corner—but she liked the simplicity of it. Much better than those new ones with the hibiscus flowers in the background. Where did they think Grayson's was, Hawaii? It made absolutely no sense. They didn't even sell flowers. Not a single one. Nothing tropical. Just local produce, organic goods, toiletries. Now that she was the manager, she would try to convince John Grayson to order a new batch, exact replicas of her own. No more of this *hello, my name is Hibiscus Flower*. Just the name, pure and simple.

She loved being manager. She felt like a parent to all these kids fresh out of high school and college, all these young people who worked the cash registers while they figured things out. They wouldn't be cashiers for long; the staff changed often, and if a bright kid lingered for too long, Ena gave them a nudge, just a nudge, and told them about all the better things out there. Sometimes they listened, and sometimes they didn't, but at least Ena tried.

She had worked longer hours at the store since her husband Renny left her. Sometimes she felt like he was still around, as though he'd died and was a ghost hidden somewhere in the floorboards. She realized that she would never know about it if he died—she wouldn't even see it in the obituaries, because he'd moved to Vancouver, B.C. with that blue-haired gypsy woman who was seven years older than her yet still, apparently, preferable. There was no coming back from Canada. There was no coming back from gypsies. Renny could well die without her even knowing about it.

+++++

"They're going to think you're snobby," Paula's boyfriend Ryan told her.

"They've known me for almost a year now."

"You need to show them how wonderful you are, babe."

Sometimes after work Ryan picked Paula up and took her out for happy hour at the Italian place on Main Street. She ordered the pasta with alfredo sauce and he ordered the puttanesca. Pictures of Elvis, faded to brown, hung dustily above each booth, and the stained-glass lights painted the waiters' faces a beige-green. It wasn't the kind of restaurant she usually liked—the ambiance was all wrong—but the food was better than any she'd tried.

"At the gym, we're all buddies," Ryan said between bites. "It doesn't even feel like work. Wouldn't it be more fun that way?"

Paula forced herself to smile. "I've got *you*, Ryan—that's enough."

"As long as you're happy." He set down his fork and lowered his lips to a half-moon. "What about your old friends? What's Gretchen been up to?"

"She moved to Cincinnati."

"And Aria?"

"She's busy with her kid. He's two now."

"So everyone's busy? Flora? Laurie? Tess?"

"Yep. Busy."

"Too busy to go out for a glass of wine? Or grab dinner?"

"Yep." She hadn't spent time with friends for months. Nights like this were enough, she told herself.

They finished two bottles of wine. Afterward they walked down Main Street until Ryan felt ready to drive. For such a big guy he couldn't hold his alcohol well. On nights like this, when they both felt light and warm, she convinced him

to go in the little shops with her, the boutiques that she used to go in with her mom, and she tried on golden blouses that clashed with her hair—things she would never usually buy—and he told her she looked like the sun.

By the time they got to the car, Paula was quieted by the memory of coming home from high school track practice to find a sun dress on her bed. It was lilac, gauzy and pastel, with quarter-length sleeves. There was no reason for it; no holiday, no school accomplishment—just a gift to celebrate the spring. She tried it on and showed her parents. As usual, her mom pretended that Paula's dad had helped her pick it out, and Paula smiled and played along.

+++++

When Ena was young, she wanted to be an

artist. She was good with water colors, and she bought her own easel with the money she saved up at her after-school job at the department store. When she graduated high school, she lived with her parents and tried to sell her paintings, but no one wanted them. It was only temporary, she told herself. She would keep practicing, keep painting, and someday she would make it big. Maybe she would go to art school.

In the meantime she kept up with her work, the same old job, sorting clothes, arranging mannequins. They promoted her to the head of the ladies department. She had less time for painting, but at least she made enough money to go out on the weekends.

Bailey's was her favorite bar. That was where she met Renny. He had long hair back then, all the way down to his shoulders, and he wore a faux leather jacket that crinkled when he moved his arms. His eyeglasses made him look eccentric.

"Can I buy you a drink?" he asked.

"It better be a strong one." She whacked his shoulder playfully. She was always doing that back then. Thought it was flirty. She told her friends she'd be right back, and she followed Renny to the counter. He ordered two shots of vodka.

"One two three," he said. They downed them together.

Renny was a poet. He'd had two poems published in the Bayside Literary Journal, and a third poem had won a contest and was going to be published in an anthology.

"If you write your own poetry book, I'll paint the illustrations to go with it. The cover, at least," Ena said.

"That might just be enough motivation for me to finish. I've got a pile of old work at home that needs editing. If I slough through that I'll send it in somewhere. See what happens."

He did finish it, and the cover was the first thing Ena had painted in months. Ena thought Renny's work was a little morose, but poetry had always been a mystery to her. His poems focused on landscapes—rocks, mostly—so she painted a cliff at sunset, all the colors metallic, but still gentle, like a glimpse of gold through water. It was one of her finest paintings. Renny sent the picture in with his manuscript.

He explained to her that it would take ages to hear back from the publishers.

"I have a good feeling about it," said Ena. "This is our big break."

But, one by one, they said no. Renny found

ENA THOUGHT RENNY'S WORK WAS A LITTLE MOROSE, BUT POETRY HAD ALWAYS BEEN A MYSTERY TO HER.

a few more publishers, and sent out updated manuscripts. Meanwhile they spent Friday nights at Bailey's, and on warm afternoons when Renny was done with his shift at the hardware store, they went for hikes up on the hill.

"This is the kind of place we need to live," she told him. "Fresh air. Trees. It's inspiring, isn't it? Being up here, on top of everything?" She was eager to move out of her parent's house. In those days she so desperately wanted Renny to propose, and when he finally did, she brought up the hill again. She loved the forest. Everywhere she looked was a new painting; a new angle of light. "There are some nice houses up there. The perfect place for two artists."

Renny was worried it would be too expensive, but they found a cheap house with a view, the paint faded, one of the doors loose from its hinges. They cleaned it up and painted it a gray-blue. Ena found some wind chimes at the thrift-store. She decorated them with oil paints, and she hung them in the trees, one by one, to remind herself that she was an artist, and that this was her place of creation.

The department store went out of business. Ena thought this was a sign that she should work on her art again. One of the girls at the store told her about a new art school about an hour's drive from town. The tuition wasn't cheap, but now that Renny had found work as an electrician, she thought they could swing it.

"I'll earn all the money back someday," she said.

"You've never sold a painting in your life."

"Not yet."

"Ena, don't you think you're getting a little too old for this? Art is an expensive hobby."

"Just because you don't write anymore doesn't mean I have to quit painting."

"Maybe you should find some steady work. How are we going to pay off the house if I'm the only one working? Things will be tight if there's tuition to pay."

WAS SHE AN ARTIST IF NO ONE WANTED HER WORK? HAD HE LIED TO HER WHEN HE SAID HER PAINTINGS WERE BEAUTIFUL?

She applied at Grayson's. At night and on weekends she tried to paint, but she kept hearing Renny's voice, again and again—*art is an expensive hobby*. That's all her paintings were to him. A hobby. Maybe that's all they had ever been. Was she an artist if no one wanted her work? Had he lied to her when he said her paintings were beautiful?

+++++

Paula stretched out on the couch. She should call her father. It had been nearly a month since she last spoke to him. He would be there all alone, sitting on his couch, hands on his belly, breathing slowly. She might go over and have dinner with him, as long as they ate at a restaurant or something. Being in that house reminded her of her mother's funeral, how they were late leaving the house, how they lingered in the hallway, their heads leaned against each other's shoulders, his suit a scratchy wool that smelled like cedar satchels meant to keep moths away.

She sat up. Tomorrow was her mother's birthday. She plucked her phone from her back pocket. It rang three times. Four times. The answering machine kicked in. *Hello, you've reached the Knapp family. We're not here right now, but leave us a message and we'll get back to you as soon as possible. Thanks!*

It startled her. Every time it startled her.

"Happy birthday," she told her mom's voice.

When she was healthy, her mom always celebrated her birthday with a hike. Some years they drove out of town, out by the coast where the air tasted like salt, and other years they stayed around and hiked up the hill trail. Wherever they went, they took a birthday picture at the most scenic point, the top of the hill or the cliff-side overlook, her and her mom, arms linked, sunburnt, windblown, and Paula sang happy birthday to her. Her dad didn't like hiking, but he met up with them later for dinner and cake. On the trail it was just the two of them. Her mom whistled along with the birds. They brought a picnic lunch—sandwiches, potato chips, and Pellegrino—and chose a sunny spot to enjoy it. All day she wore the little plastic birthday crown that Paula gave her when she was a little girl.

She called back and listened to the voice again. Last year on her mother's birthday, Paula spent the entire day on her couch, paralyzed, unsure what to make of the world. Her mom would hate to find out that she hadn't hiked. She'd want Paula to celebrate her birthday just like they always had, out on the trail. Maybe this year. Maybe tomorrow.

+++++

Today was Saturday, but Ena couldn't sleep. She stepped outside—still in her house shoes— buttoned up her corduroy jacket, and stared hard at the lower world. She lived in a clearing at the top of the hill. The forest spread out beneath her, much like a night-washed sea. Beyond the forest, the town sprawled, weak and pale, the color of sand. There was Grayson's. The library. Main Street, with its boutiques and restaurants. She could see it all from up here, except the people. They were too small and too sandy to see.

Her wind chimes rang. They were gray now. Metal inside. Stained, splintering wood. All the paint had chipped away.

She wondered why she didn't move. She could imagine a new life in some clean little house down in the valley, somewhere with a lawn and a bed of tulips. A house all her own; no ghosts to share it with.

+++++

Paula set out with the backpack she used for day hikes, the small one with the built-in water bottle. A few drops leaked down her back when she walked quickly enough. It had always been like that; a faulty design, a cheap brand, but she used it anyway because her mother had gotten it for her when she graduated college. It made her feel hollow to think how much happier she'd been back then. But she forgot all this for a moment, as she took off from the trailhead. Dawn was creaking open. The clouds spread high over the hill, revealing a solid beam of light. Miraculous, Paula thought. Absolutely miraculous.

She always hoped to see deer on cool mornings like this. Most people thought of them as pests because of their affinity for garden vegetables, but Paula thought that was unfair. They were just being deer. She loved their smoky, long-lashed eyes; that glassy spot in the middle of the pupil that looked like a calm, winter lake. The trees hushed around her in one long ripple. She heard wind chimes, a glittering mix of bamboo and metal going up in scale. They reminded her of her parents' house, all those wind chimes on the porch and in the cottonwood trees, billowing like the tentacles of jellyfish, around and around. Paula stopped for a moment to catch her breath and to listen. She had always been jealous of the people who lived near this trail. They must go hiking every day. They must wake up early and watch the sun rise over the valley, glad to be alive.

+++++

When the sun had risen, Ena sat on her deck to bask in the light with a cup of sharp, black tea. She didn't know what to do with her weekends anymore. If her knee wasn't so bad she might go for a hike or a bicycle ride, but those days were long over.

Just as she was thinking about whether or not to plant the first crop of nasturtiums in her garden, a doe wandered in. Usually she yelled at deer, a stout *get!*, but this one looked straight at her. Against the light, Ena could see every wiry hair on the deer's back, stroked smooth, like damp pine needles, like beargrass. The white spots on her rump were cow-like, creamy. It was only a fawn, Ena realized. Where was the mother?

Suddenly, a girl wandered in as well. She was slender, athletic looking, dressed in leggings and hiking boots. Evidently she hadn't seen the signs. Ena and her neighbors had petitioned the city for years to put those up. Some good that did. "Excuse me. This is private property," Ena yelled. The deer took a few steps forward but didn't flee, even with the suddenness of her voice.

"I'm so sorry," the girl said in a loud whisper. Then she pointed at the deer, as though this would explain everything.

The woman gestured for Paula to come up on the deck. For a moment Paula felt like a child about to be scolded, but then she remembered that she was, in fact, an adult. She stepped quietly next to the woman—older, almost completely gray haired, with just a few long cat-stripes of brown left next to her ears. She smelled like her mother, like baby lotion, and Paula found herself hot and itchy, exploded from within with the helium that prefaces tears.

Why was this girl sniffling? Ena thought. Allergies? She glanced over and realized she was crying. The girl wasn't even trying to hide it, but let the tears ride down her cheeks. Was she crying over the deer? Its unsure future? Its sweet, heart-shaped nose? Ena didn't know how to ask, so she handed the girl her handkerchief. Renny used to make fun of her for carrying one, but it came in handy at a time like this.

Paula dried her face. For some reason she wasn't embarrassed. The woman patted her arm and was kind enough not to say anything about the strangeness of it. The baby deer sniffed around. Its muscles showed no fear, no hurry.

The fawn ate some of Ena's violets. She'd been wanting to move them to another bed, anyway. It was kind of nice to have the company, the deer and the girl both, and when at last the fawn sprung off, leaping high over bushes and fallen branches, Ena thought that the poor thing might just make it on its own.

With the deer gone, Paula thought of all the things she could say to the woman, the thank you's and the explanations, but she worried that

that would ruin the softness of the moment. It was still just after dawn. The light wrapped through the cottonwood trees, their heart-shaped leaves glowing a translucent, papery green. Paula had never seen cottonwoods on the hill. She thought again of home. One day, when she was very little, her mother set up a blanket for a special picnic. They sat beneath the cottonwoods, in the summer shade, the yard still fragrant with water from the garden hose. Mist rose from the lawn, just barely, little droplets evaporating in the sun. Her mother handed her a still-cold juice box, and saltines pressed with peanut butter. "You hear that, Paula?" her mother said. She looked up at the trees. The wind bent through each leaf, all of them wooshing, all of them turning. "These are wind trees." She smiled at Paula, then, the softest of all smiles which, like her hugs, and like her very gaze, meant everything was alright, had always been, would always be. "The best of all my wind chimes."

Paula cleared her throat and took a deep breath. "Did you plant those? Those cottonwoods?" she asked the woman.

"My husband did," Ena said. "Years ago." He'd heard it was best to plant trees at the end of winter, and so he spent all afternoon in the blank, March wind, breaking through the soil with a shovel. She'd stood at the window and sipped her tea. He hadn't asked for her help and she hadn't offered, but she'd made sure to tell him that they were beautiful trees, their silver bark composed of both shadows and sunlight, their buds soon to become pure, absolute movement.

"They're beautiful," the girl said.

Ena nodded. "Especially on a day like today."

The girl was adjusting her backpack, getting ready to leave. Ena wanted to know why she'd cried. She realized how long it had been since anyone had stood on this deck with her.

"Would you like some tea, dear?" the woman asked. She motioned to a set of deck chairs, and a small table with a porcelain teapot. "The water's probably still hot."

"Sure," Paula said. She owed the woman an explanation for trespassing, and, anyway, the woman's voice was kind.

Ena led her into the kitchen. She hadn't given the place a good cleaning in a while, but this girl didn't seem like the type who would judge her for dusty baseboards or a ring of bread crumbs around the toaster.

"Black, green, or white?"

"Do you have any herbal?"

"Herbal?"

"Mint? Or hibiscus?"

"I have green tea mixed with lemon. Take it or leave it."

Paula laughed. "That sounds perfect."

They sat on the deck, on crafty chairs made from what looked like willow branches. "Did you make these?" Paula asked.

"Yes," Ena said, even though she'd really only made one of them, during a crafting class at the community college some years ago. That was the closest she'd come to painting again. Renny found the other chair at a yard sale; the bark matched exactly, that purple-brown of dried wood. They were a perfect match. Renny should've taken the chairs with him. She didn't want them anymore. Maybe she would give them away and buy some new chairs with her employee discount at Grayson's.

"They're beautiful." Paula sipped her tea. "How do you bend branches like that?"

"You soak them. Just a few hours, and then they're ready to bend."

Paula nodded. She wasn't sure what to say next. This was something that happened more often as she got older. It seemed that her mind was sometimes just empty of ideas, empty of thoughts and words and filled only with images. Memories danced around her in slow, leaking colors, somewhere between sepia and black-and-white. Despite their dimness, these memories felt more real than the present moment—here, in this body, here, now—and more real than words.

She tried to talk about this with Ryan. They'd been together since before her mother's diagnosis. He was there for everything, her mother's entire sickness and death, and yet, somehow, he still didn't understand. He couldn't—it wasn't his mother who'd died. He'd never lost anyone he loved. Whenever Paula cried, Ryan tried to console her. He patted her back with the muscular palms of his hands, and whispered *shh*. He nodded as she spoke, but when she tried to talk about emptiness, or about the movement of time, he said "you are so smart, babe" or "hey, that's interesting", and the conversation ended there. His memories were just memories, and that was all. One night when she was staying over at his house, she asked if the memories ever took over. If he ever felt like he was falling, every joyous moment behind him, in the clouds, in the air, and nothing but death below. "Paula, I don't know," he said. "Ask me later." She asked him again the next weekend, and he said, "I don't know what to tell you. It's past midnight, aren't you ready for bed yet?"

He turned over then and she could hear that his breathing was still fast, and awake. He pretended to sleep for a few minutes and then he said, "Babe, I'm worried about you."

+++++

This girl's a quiet one, Ena thought. Maybe this would end up like a conversation with Irma Jean, that woman at work who sat silent or chewed on cookies while Ena did all the talking. "Do you live in the valley?" Ena asked.

It turned out they worked only a few blocks down from each other. Paula had likely seen her at the check-out counter when, all those years ago, Ena started out as a cashier.

"Isn't it funny how we're around people all the time and we don't even know them?" Ena said. "You can walk past someone every day of your life without even knowing who they are."

"I would've never known. How is it, living up here? Do you love it?"

"I liked it better when I could move around a bit easier. But the view is nice." The girl gave her a look like—that's it? That's all you can say about it? Ena went on: "There's just a lot of memories attached to this house. Some good. Some bad. Some that won't leave me alone. Most of them

SHE WASN'T SURE WHAT TO SAY NEXT. THIS WAS SOMETHING THAT HAPPENED MORE OFTEN AS SHE GOT OLDER.

about my ex-husband." She hadn't shared this much of herself in a long time. This girl was easy to talk to. She told her everything; the whole divorce, the emptiness at night, when the lights were off and she could hear nothing but the spinning of the Earth.

"Did you ever think of moving?"

"Sure. But—it's a tough decision. I've spent most of my life collecting memories here."

"Do you think it's possible to get lost in them?"

"Lost in memories?"

Paula nodded. She wished she hadn't said anything; she never knew quite how to explain it. A feeling that the past was better than the present or future could be. She told Ena about her mother's breast cancer, her slow withering, her death.

Ena felt horrible for this poor young thing. Life was a bubble. Ready to pop. One day you're fine, the next day you're gone, just like that. She spoke carefully. "The way I look at it is: if I lose the bad memories, then I'll lose the good ones, too." Yes. That was why she hadn't moved. This was the house she came to as an artist. Those were her wind chimes. "What are you going to do with your life, girl? When you get tired of that boring job of yours?" Ena asked.

"I don't know. I have no idea."

"What's your dream?"

"I don't think I have one."

"Find it. Search for it." Ena told the girl her story; how she'd wanted so desperately to be an artist. How she gave up on it. How the last thing she painted were those cottonwood trees, their leaves in flight, the sun shining in behind them. When she finished, she'd left the painting on the easel for days. Renny never said one word about it. He walked past it every day and he never even stopped to look. "Time goes by faster than you can imagine," Ena said.

"I know." The girl began to cry again. Her tears were completely silent. Water over stone. "You think that deer will be alright?" the girl asked, suddenly.

"I think so. She seemed like a sturdy young thing." Ena paused.

"Yeah, she did."

+++++

It was noon by the time they said good-bye, but Paula hiked the rest of the hill. She was glad to return to the trail. The shadows stretched in front of her, wind-blown, long and shifting as grasses beneath the sea. They moved with her. Her shadow, too, changed as the wind carved through it. In some places she couldn't tell the difference; her hair looked so much like branches, and her torso was cylindrical, like a trunk. Shadow on top of shadow.

Ena invited her to lunch on Monday. They were going to meet at Grayson's, and then walk to the café down the street, the one with the yellow umbrellas out front.

She heard Ena's voice repeating: "What do you want to do with your life?"

THAT WAS WHY SHE HADN'T MOVED. THIS WAS THE HOUSE SHE CAME TO AS AN ARTIST. THOSE WERE HER WIND CHIMES.

AT THE TOP OF THE HILL, THE WORLD SPILLED DOWN BENEATH HER, ALL BROWN AND BLUE AND CREAMY WHITE, WASHED CLEAN AND COLD BY THE MORNING.

What *did* she want to do with her life? Usually when this question came into her head Paula pushed it away, but now she couldn't stop thinking about it. She didn't know what kind of job she wanted, but she knew she didn't want to work in insurance. Maybe it was finally time to consider moving on. No, more than that. Suddenly she felt itchy about it. She didn't want to stay there another day. Not one more day. She'd always hated that job and she only took it because her parents encouraged her to.

This would probably worry Ryan. "Babe, you can't just quit your job like that. You have to give notice."

True—but she didn't want to wait. She didn't want to wait any longer.

"Are you sure you've thought this through?"

Paula sometimes wondered why Ryan hadn't proposed. She wondered if she would say yes. That was another thought she usually pushed away.

At the top of the hill, the world spilled down beneath her, all brown and blue and creamy white, washed clean and cold by the morning. And what a crazy morning, Paula thought. She took off her backpack and sat in the sun, in that magnificent beam of light. "Happy birthday, Mom," she said, and she sang to her. ⬤

Words by Joel Preston Smith

Artwork by Brianna Spencer

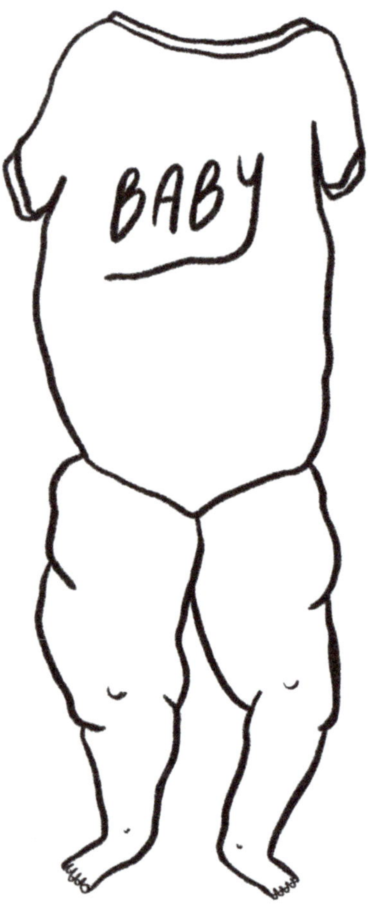

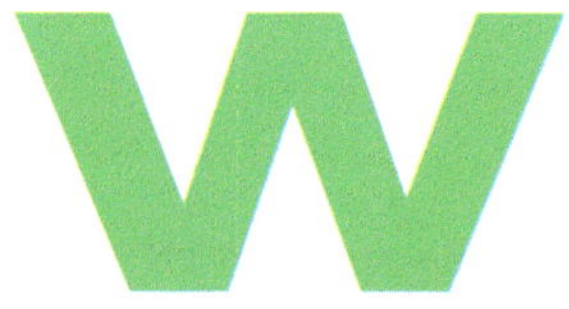

We were on opposite sides of the onesies rack at Target. You asked me my opinion of a onesie that said I HATE MY THIGHS. I said I thought it seemed kind of sexist and it was wrong to start a kid out freaked out about body image but the color (Tigger striped, with Pooh Bear shaped crotch snaps) was OK. You said maybe it was supposed to be satirical, like maybe it was poking fun at how ridiculous it is we're like all drowning in this constant fear we're not tall enough, thin enough, with flawless skin and perfect teeth (speak for yourself, lol).

I said what if it isn't? What if someone's truly dumb enough to dress some poor kid in basically what amounts to their own pre-conceived notion that being a fat little cute baby isn't perfectly acceptable and might even be perfectly normal? I mean, what are the parents supposed to do, buy it a stair-stepper?

You seemed confused but then I pointed out that the good thing was that whenever the kid looked at herself in a mirror the sign was going to be upside down and backwards anyway, so unless the baby was Chinese (which all seem to be born geniuses at least in math and nobody puts math equations on onesies, which if you think about it is another way of narrowing babies minds) it probably would just think it had thrown up on itself, so there's that.

I also pointed out that in some countries with limited internet access where probably Vogue and Cosmopolitan (and maybe even Ladies Home Journal too) are banned, like North Korea and Libya, and way back when, it's perfectly normal to eat whatever you want whenever you want and no one in their right mind is going to hold you up to some imperialist viewpoint of morbid obesity (partly I suppose because you can't be seen under those acres and acres of black cloth anyway), so even though they make these shirts underground in giant sweatshops I doubt anybody there would dare wear one (I don't think they write them in Arabian anyway and even if they did it would be invisible under the blanket thing).

You said you were late for a meeting. I was sorry I didn't get to hear your other opinion. Let's keep arguing lol! Drinks? Coffee? The clearance rack at Wal-Mart lol? Btw I was just shopping for my sister-in-law who just had a baby. I don't have any children at the moment. P.S. I liked the one with the outline of a raccoon that said TRASH PANDA better. You should go for that one instead. ⓑ

Following spread: Alyson Provax, 2019

it could have been worse could have been worse could have been worse it

you know you know you know you know you know you know you know you know

into this absence
into this absence
into this absence
into this absence
into this absence
into this absence
into this absence

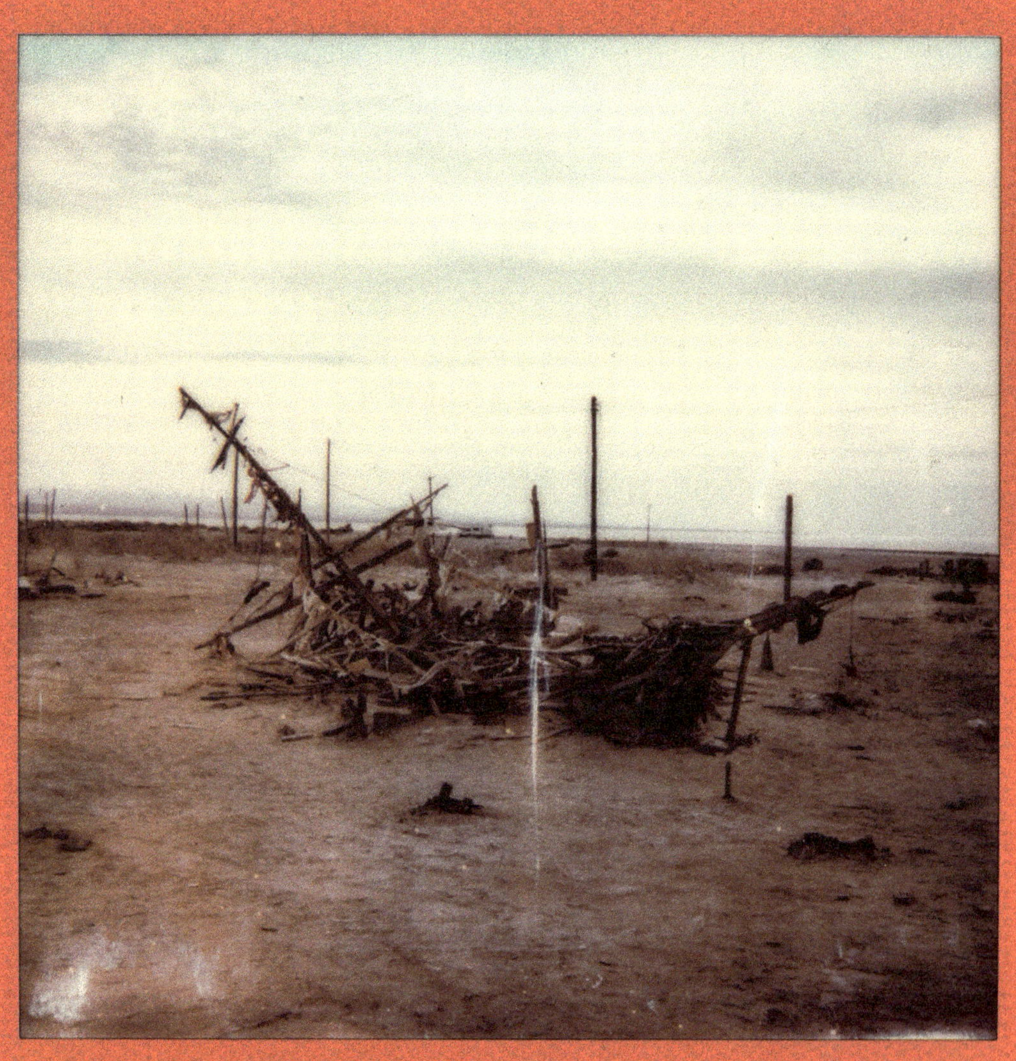

THEY COME FROM THE VOID

Words by Luke Elliott

Artwork by Mike Vos

Luke Elliott has a B.A. in Creative Writing and an MFA in Writing Popular Fiction. In 2017, he launched the *Ink to Film* podcast where he discusses books and their film adaptations from a craft perspective with his filmmaker co-host. In 2018, he earned a spot in the Viable Paradise writers' workshop where he studied with well-known writers in the SF/F field. Recently, his short fiction was selected for the *Best Vegan Science Fiction and Fantasy of 2018* collection. In his free time, he collects quality whiskies and is always happy to pour a dram for company.

Orblights rose from beneath black waves, boiling the saltwater into white banks of steam. Seven lighthouses flashed golden as their rotating lenses cut beams from the headland into the rolling sea. The orblights hovered over shoals, between craggy sea stacks, and amid high breaking surf in paths unwavering, though the sea assailed them. They would only alter course to glide up the sheer cliffs into the coastal village of Overmorn Cove, whose people congregated outside their homes to meet them.

Marie, wrapped in a knit seafoam shawl matching her dyed hair, waited on a cliff overlooking the coast. Shawl and hair both lashed in the wind about her face, fluttering against her cheeks. Her toes touched the precipice, breaking tiny rocks off to cascade into the void. She stood with shoulders back–chin and jaw fixed as she waited, watching the otherworldly things come, so bright they darkened the stars beyond.

Five nights running Marie had dreamt of

being taken, of being swallowed whole. An orblight melted into her bedroom, lowering itself over where she lay paralyzed, breath clipped and shallow. It stopped an inch above her nose, looming until she could see nothing else, sense nothing else. It incinerated her with light.

"Come back," her husband called.

Marie gazed at the rocky shore hundreds of feet below and swayed as a swell of vertigo knotted her insides. She imagined her body cracking against the black stones, only to rise up and smash against them again, tumbling over and over amid the breaking waves.

An orblight glided into view, coasting up the cliff directly underneath. She strode away from the cliff and through their flimsy fence to rejoin her anxious husband, who waited for her on their small lawn.

"One's coming," she said.

He shut his eyes and inhaled through his nose. "Camphor. I can smell it."

She sniffed. Only sap, brine, and loam. She took Gavon's familiar and calloused hand as the pale orblight crested the cliff like a moonrise come to Earth.

"Look, Marie," Gavon said. "It *is* divine."

+++++

As one of forty-two keepers in town, Marie's job was to tend the old-style lamp in Duskbridge, westernmost tower of the seven. She and Mrs. Linscomb, her partner on Tuesdays and Thursdays, were to ensure it never extinguished during their shift.

That morning, a spider had spun up a new web in one corner of the entry chamber in the base of the tower, with rings of thickly bound strands forming wide erratic gaps in the web. She fetched a broom.

"You're a weird little bug-eater, you know that?" she said to the empty spaces where such creatures tucked themselves away. The web glinted with faint moisture, its owner absent the delicate strands. "That's probably the worst web I've ever seen." One reminiscent of the images you might find online of spiders who'd spun erratic patterns after researchers exposed them to different drugs.

"What's that?" Mrs. Linscomb shouted down. The Duskbridge tower stood only a couple stories tall as the squattest of the seven.

"Just yammering to myself." The broom fit neatly back on its rack. She could always clear it tomorrow. She shouldered her bag and walked over to the wrought-iron spiral staircase to climb to her post, but froze, foot hovering above the first step.

Gaps in the web were self-sabotage.

Her foot returned to the floor. The spider did not seem to realize what they'd done–it had worked hard at the web oblivious to the problem. What if holes impaired her, too, but she didn't notice them?

She studied the skin on the backs of her hands for holes, which she found, if only the typical pores. Nothing larger, at least that she could perceive.

SHE STUDIED THE SKIN ON THE BACKS OF HER HANDS FOR HOLES, WHICH SHE FOUND, IF ONLY THE TYPICAL PORES.

She collected her knitting needles and the shawl she'd been working at for a month, preparing to climb up to her post.

Her hand froze. She trembled as she lifted

her shawl for a better look. Quarter-sized holes dotted the pattern.

"I'm actually not feeling well today," she shouted up to Mrs. Linscomb. "I thought I could shake this bug in a day, but it seems the worst is yet to come. I'm going home. Phone over to the church and let Father Elo know if you want."

Mrs. Linscomb's white ponytail dangled over the railing, followed by her flushed, froggy face as she peered down through the space between the stairs. "If I want?" she said. "I *have* to contact Father Elo—nobody's allowed to keep watch alone."

Marie shoved the shawl to the bottom of her bag. Let some strange ship wander into their damned secret. Tonight, the orblights would take her. Just as they'd taken her sister. And even Father Elo, full of righteous rage, couldn't excommunicate one of the Transcended. Or the dead, for that matter. She cleared her things from her locker and unplugged her radio.

"You don't seem ill," Mrs. Linscomb said.

Marie put her palm to her forehead, maybe a little too fast. "I'm really queasy. Honestly, I might hurl. I wouldn't want you to have to clean vomit."

That did it.

"You're gosh-darn right I'm not cleaning that up! You throw up and that's on you—I don't care if you're too weak to lift a mop." Mrs. Linscomb's wide face disappeared from above, her trailing ponytail last to go.

Marie shut the lighthouse door behind her and trudged away, bag overfull and heavy, making her every footfall sink into the mud down the path from the tower. A misting rain salted her lips with brine carried from the shore. The soil clung to her shoes, swallowing the soles. It squelched as she fought to be free with every

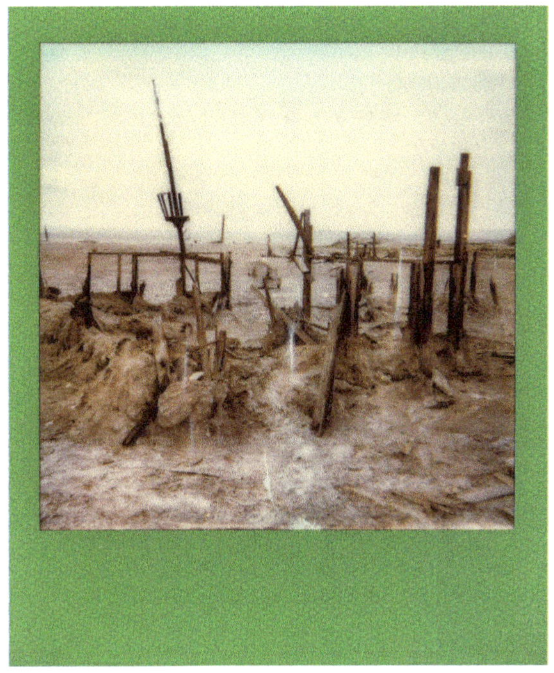

step. A woodpecker hammered away, burrowing into the trunk.

+++++

Gavon came through their front door as he usually did, already complaining about his work. "Another fifty marked for cut and burn today. The wood's all unusable, just like the others. Whatever is plaguing the forest around here is just getting—"

"It comes from them," Marie said. She sat leafing through a worn leather-bound photo album at the center of their living room carpet.

He didn't speak, but his rigid body-language did. She didn't have to sniff to know he'd smell like pine resin, sawdust, and gym clothes in need of a wash.

"There's something wrong with it all," she announced, as if only to the world. "Holes in the spiderwebs, mold-formations, rotting trees, relentless woodpeckers — how haven't you noticed?"

125

He ignored her, dropped his duffel full of safety gear on the bench by the door, hooked his jacket over a coat hook, and stepped into the kitchen, boots clomping. The cupboard hinge squeaked as he rummaged for the coffee grounds. His throat worked as he started a pot brewing, as if silently testing responses.

"My own knitting, Gav." She balled her shawl up and tossed it into the kitchen.

He scooped it up and examined it, peering through the cluster of openings at her. "I don't get it, what's wrong with it?"

"I didn't intend to make it that way. Holes were in the spider's web earlier, too."

He set the shawl on the table and leaned against the flaking kitchen countertop. "Sounds like you're having an episode again…"

"I don't need meds," she said, voice rising. "I'm fine. It's this place, these *things*, that are off–making us go wrong."

His finger picked at the yellow flakes, freeing them, but only widening the exposed particle board beneath. Dried blood crusted beneath his nails. "We're not having this conversation again. Father Elo says that questions only weaken our bond. And dammit, Marie, you know we're supposed to report it to the elders if we hear voiced doubts. Even from family."

"You say my name like it's gone sour in your mouth."

He pulled his favorite mug out of the cabinet, which read "lumberjacks do it in the woods."

His broad frame loomed even larger in the compact kitchen than usual from her vantage point, sitting cross-legged on the threadbare carpet. Like a child who'd nearly outgrown their playhouse.

Her hand lingered on an old Polaroid from senior prom, tracing her teenage smile with a fingertip. They'd both been a lot thinner back then, her a near waif, him a stick-bug in boy form swallowed by a rented tuxedo. Mixed-race couples still drew loaded stares back then, and perhaps they still did, and she'd just grown accustomed to the way people gawked at them.

A scatter of brown mildew dotted the margins of the open page.

The coffee pot's chime broke minutes of silence. Gavon filled his mug. "I refuse to report my own wife. Rules be damned." A shocking phrase, coming from him. "But you should go to the elders. You miss your sisters–that's all this is–grief. No way you're disfellowshipped for grief."

"That's not all it is." Marie blew a seafoam lock of hair out of her eyes, only to have it droop right back into place. "I've never told you, but the orblights always terrified me. Even as a child. Ever since they came for my granddad."

She plucked at a strand of their fraying carpet, which uprooted and made things worse.

"I used to collect loose buttons to give him," she said. "Like prizes. He'd ooh and ahh, as if I'd presented gemstones instead of rubbish. Tell me he'd treasure them forever."

YOU SAY MY NAME LIKE IT'S GONE SOUR IN YOUR MOUTH.

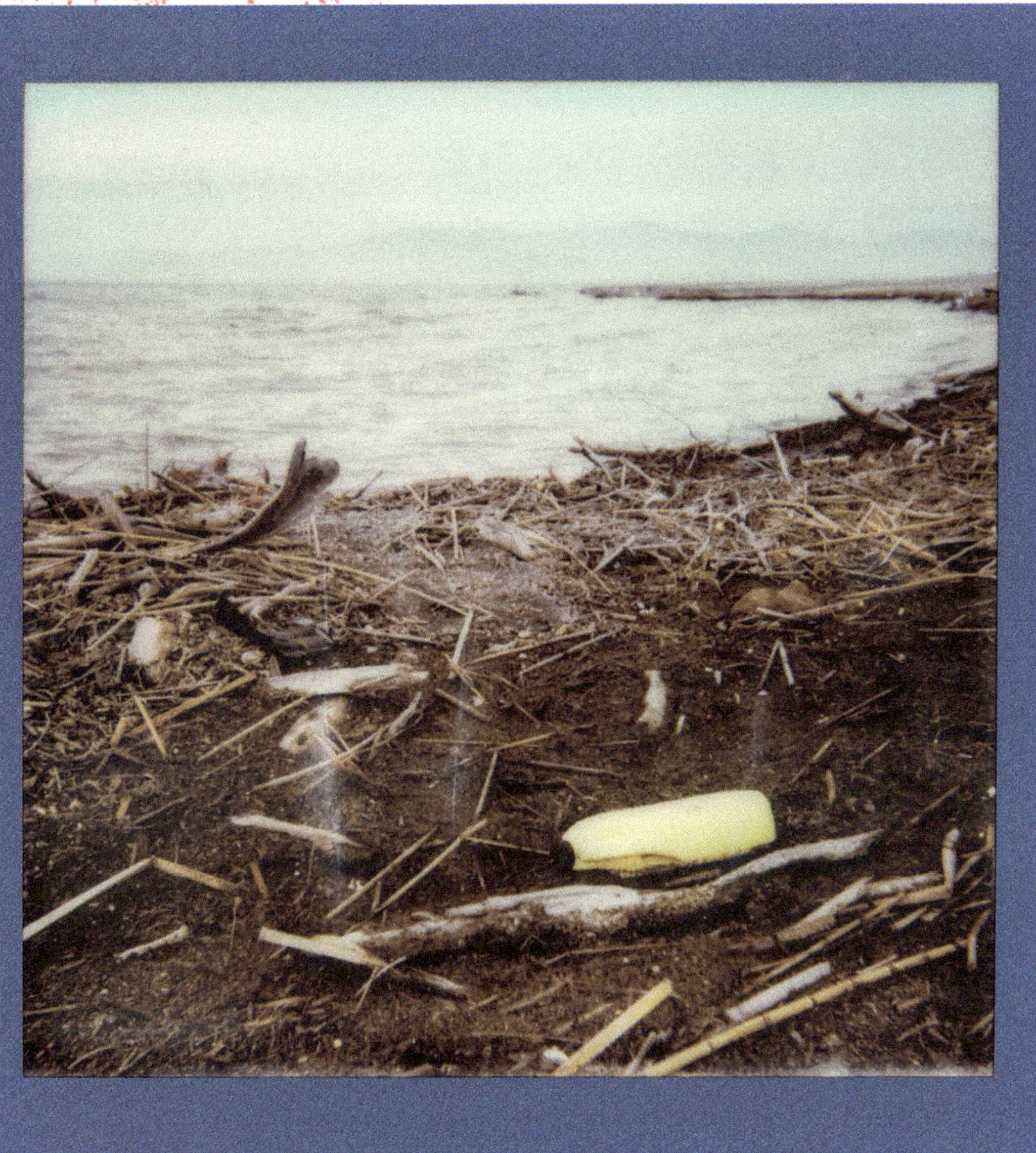

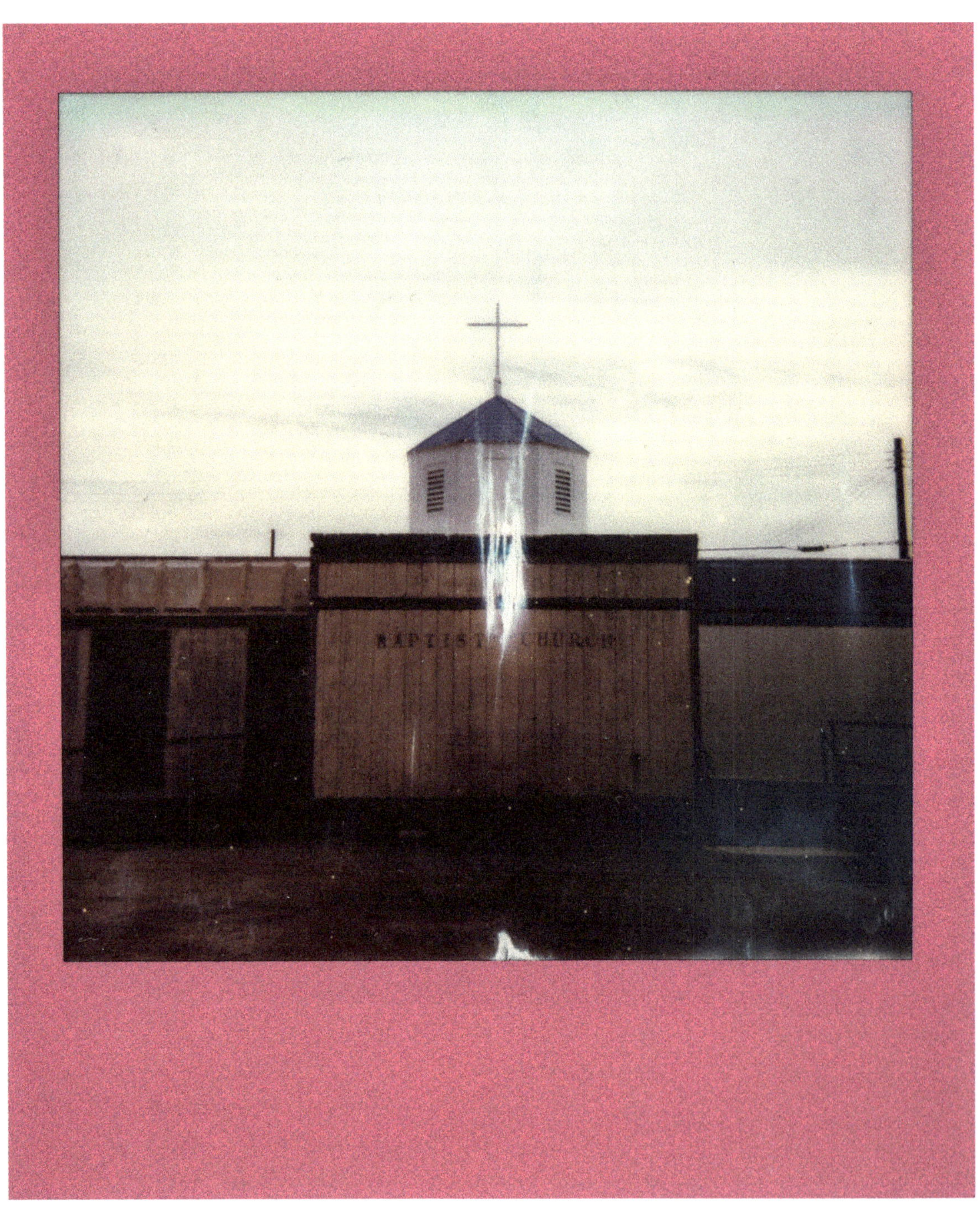

BAPTIST CHURCH

"Sounds like a good man." He sipped his coffee. "I wish I'd known him."

"After the orblights took him, I rebelled. Stopped praying. Stopped eating. Mother forced me to go to twice the daily scripture readings. Losing my sisters only confirmed what I knew even then, as a confused little girl."

"If you tell Father Elo—"

"I could be stoned to death."

Gavon hurled his half-full coffee mug and she flinched, raising her arms to cover her face. It collided with the frame for the opening between rooms, exploding into ceramic shards that skittered across the linoleum.

When he spoke next, his voice rattled through a cage of teeth. "You don't give a shit about me, do you?" He stabbed a finger toward her.

Marie shut the photo album, slid it back into the bookshelf, and stood, calmly. "Of course I do, Gav." She went to him, putting a hand on his arm. His tension eased and he wrapped her in an apologetic hug.

Rivulets of coffee ran down the curling wallpaper, leaving a fresh stain of grasping tendrils. He trembled, rocking her in his arms in a gentle sway. "I'll stand beside you tonight. Despite this." He kissed her neck. "You'll come to see them as I do and repent. In the morning, we'll go to the elders together and cleanse your soul."

She pulled back, holding him at arm's length. "And if I'm taken?"

Gavon extracted himself from her hold and pulled the dustbin out from beneath the sink and began to carefully sweep bits of broken mug into it with his bare hand. "Then you better hope the orblights are capable of forgiveness."

+++++

The sphere before her warmed to orange, then crimson as ribbons of light spread from its core. It hovered toward their fence, a hum like a vibrating cell phone heating Marie's bones, stirring her insides. She had left the gate open, but the orblight floated through the fencerow instead, melting it as if it were wax, and not moldy old pine.

Heat drove away the chill of the ocean wind as it crossed the lawn. She shivered.

Gavon squeezed her hand harder. Painfully hard.

Still crimson, but reeking blue, the orblight stopped paces away. Its luminance flickered in sliding patches. The ill-defined edge of the sphere stayed impossible to distinguish. It radiated warmth, but carried emotion too, wrapped around it in a nimbus.

The peace of a summer morning spent basking in the sun on a porch swing cascaded over her. She chomped her tongue, drawing blood until the pain and metallic tinge banished the invading tranquility.

The people of Overmorn Cove yearned to be chosen. Devotees shed tears of exultation, even as their only child "Transcended." The old church, a sea-weathered steeple on the edge of the cliff, had long ago been cleansed of Christian icons. Stripped after the orblights first rose from the sea. Jesus, Allah, and Buddha fell from walls and mantelpieces as people cast aside their old faiths in reverence for the new.

The boulder-sized crimson orblight inched closer, commanding her attention as blades of grass flattened beneath it, laid low by its aura. A sharp odor filled the air like burning wire.

She thrust her chin forward. "Take me then, damn you."

Gavon crushed her palm in a plea to stop blaspheming. She tore her gaze for a moment from the orblight. Tears wet her husband's dark cheeks, gleaming in the strange brilliance.

A corona spread from the orblight's center, separating into coils of light and lifting from an inner nucleus. They waggled through the air in all directions, each moving as if with independent sentience. Where the coils licked the grass the blades melted, like artificial turf instead of brittle organics.

The tendrils of bodied light snaked forward, enwrapping them both. Warmth and joy, pure and horrifying, infused her every thought. Gavon's clothes sublimated into black vapor and were carried away on the wind.

The tendrils withdrew their grasp, leaving her alone in the cold.

Gavon's naked form diminished as he disappeared through its outer horizon, vanishing into the unknown space within.

Transcended.

The orblight retreated, retracing its path as she struggled to breathe through the anguish.

Gavon had craved this moment. Prayed for it. The elderly in Overmorn Cove lived their entire lives without being chosen, often dying instead in sickbeds with silent screams on their lips, terrified of the void. Her granddad had been "lucky" to be spared that fate. Gavon's own father had not, succumbing instead to the horrors of disease.

But her heart hurt like a spear had plunged through her chest. What if they chose Gavon to punish her?

She charged, screaming.

It accelerated as it glided toward the cliff. She ran faster, closing the distance, legs pistoning. It slipped over the precipice, but she ran on. She breathed deep and leapt, sailing out over the rocky beach two hundred feet below with arms cast wide.

And fell into the glowing thing from the sea.

+++++

Was this how a womb felt for the unborn? Dark horizons alive with strands of shadow. Warmth and comfort in thick humidity. A sweet, unnamable odor in her nose.

A being floated in the pool of an inner umbra. Humanlike, with its naked back to her. She moved toward it, unsure of how she did so. His back—she could tell he was a man now, showed brown skin glowing.

"I'm glad you came, Marie," a voice said. Gavon's voice. And yet, one not his own. It echoed in harmony with itself.

"What has it done to you?" Marie said.

"All is entwined. Comfort overwhelms despair."

He rotated to face her, feet coming to rest on a carpet of shade. He strode toward her, skin luminous, eyes alight with a nacreous shimmer.

She balled her fists, her nails cutting into her palms. "What do you want?"

"To rescue you from ceasing to be."

Marie shook her head, seafoam hair lifting buoyant about her head as if she floated in the deep end of a swimming pool. She thrust her chin forward. "Your very presence disrupts our existence. I've witnessed it."

He laid a hand atop her own. A rush of sight, sound, touch, smell, taste, and something else, an essence of pure emotion, flooded her every fiber. The birth of the cold, rocky world. A collision, and slow formation of a moon caught by that world's influence. The shaky steps of the first crocodilian creature emerging from a primal sea on flippers able to lift them from the dirt, and its sudden decay as orblights observed from above. Ice ages, violent storms, darkness, and light. Cycles of life churning away, rising and falling with ages, the orblights ever present.

Brightly feathered behemoths lumbered through verdant jungles gone in a flash. From insects to mammoths, iguanas to albatrosses, the living rose from the ashes. Finally, came apes, backs bent, then unbent. Fire and acrid smoke of their own making. Technology, the timeless lust for advancement. Fear, anguish, and even love arriving with a radiant spark.

She gasped as the rush ended at this moment. This meeting. She'd only glimpsed a bare fraction, yet she'd seen more than a life ever could, filling her mind to bursting.

"All along," she said. "You've been here all along."

It did not respond.

What of the countless holes left in the world? Millennia of rot and decay as they hovered, watching, taking.

The thing that was no longer her husband spoke with many voices. "We are multitudes. We will be all. Your Gavon makes us more in his freedom from nonexistence. Do you see?"

"The void frightens me, too, even though I came from it. We all did, before our birth."

The thing's pearlescent eyes conveyed nothing. Distant pulses of light beat somewhere beyond ropes of shadow.

"Nonexistence is the enemy," it said, voice transforming. Her granddad's white mustache sprouted across Gavon's lip as its visage shifted, wrinkling into a face she hadn't seen since she'd been a child bearing buttons. "It is your turn to escape," it said with her granddad's voice. "Hug me again, my dear, and find the end to your fear."

Tears floated out from her eyes in tiny undulating spheres to hang in a shining cluster about their heads. She met its gaze. Her answer came quickly, though she knew she might live to regret it. "I'd rather die than live as a mote of light lost in an eternal star."

He dropped his arms, as if saddened, or at least wearing a mask of someone saddened. And then it was no longer anyone.

+++++

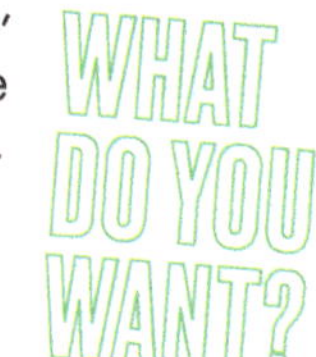

Marie opened her eyes. Hadn't they been open?

She rocked in low surf, soaked, cold, her backside skidding on stony sand.

The orblight floated away from her and out to sea. It joined the others and coalesced, as always, into a single radiant sphere that dipped beneath the waves in a geyser of steam. Gradually, the indifferent stars returned to the night.

"I hope you found peace, Gav," she whispered.

She stood in the shallow seawater and trudged back toward shore, clothes laden, shawl missing. A group of people waited on the beach as she came ashore. How long had she been inside the thing?

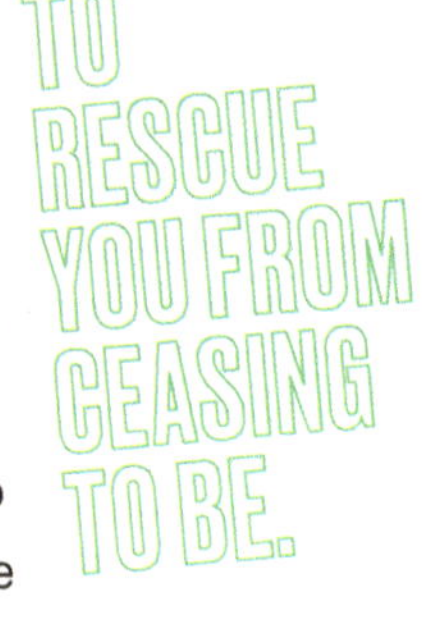

Sheriff Harrison stood among them, his long flashlight sweeping the waves as people shouted her name. A sensible man, she'd always thought, church going, but no zealot. His light fell on her as she trudged out of the waves, as if some ancient thing from the deep herself clambering ashore.

Father Elo, in full robes, waved a book of scripture around like a machine gun at everyone assembled. But the group stood transfixed by her, instead of the priest. They whispered to one another as she approached, dripping.

A rotting spar of driftwood cracked and startled the crowd as it fell to the sand.

"There she is," an elderly woman said, pointing, finger trembling. Mrs. Linscomb, Marie realized, her partner that morning at the lighthouse. "She threw herself off the cliff into one of the Holy."

The sheriff met her in the surf, his flashlight still shining in her face. "Marie Loncaster?"

Marie squinted and raised a hand to block the beam. "In the flesh."

He lowered the light. "There's a lot of folks wanting to speak with you."

"What did you see?" someone shouted from the back.

"She didn't see shit," another said. "Fell in the water–that's all."

Father Elo glared. "Do not believe a word from this deceiver!" He trembled with ire.

The crashing waves filled Marie's ears and their rhythm rocked in her stomach. How could she hope to explain something she didn't understand herself? She toppled forward onto her hands and knees in the sand and expelled what seemed a gallon of seawater. Motes of light like luminous sand fleas flickered in her sick, only to disappear into burrows in the sand.

The sheriff's hand looped under her armpit, helping her to her feet. She stared at the sand,

but the lights had gone.

"Clear a path!" he called.

The crowd parted, but people murmured to each other as she passed. Ahead, the flashing blue and red of a police cruiser colored the night. Her feet cut the beach with ease.

She stopped shy of the car and turned to the growing crowd. "I spoke to one." Her voice came loud and firm, but she didn't shout.

Their eyes shone in the reflection of the police car's lights, a sea of tiny flashing orbs themselves as they waited for someone to say something more.

"Lies," Elo shouted, and others took up the call.

Eventually, the crowd quieted again, even Elo. She thrust out her chin and spoke. "They only wish to consume you."

The sound from the people of Overmorn began as a sharp intake of collective breath,

then rose into a discordant wave of shouting and wailing. Black swells lapped in the shallows in bizarre accompaniment. The seven lighthouses fell dark, one after another, as the first hint of dawn seeped into the night. People either peeled off from the whole and wandered away or cried together as Father Elo fell to his knees in anguish. They huddled around him, comforting, seeking comfort.

The sheriff helped her into the back of the police cruiser and shut her in.

"They're going to want blood for that," he said, turning the ignition.

She kept silent as they pulled away from

AND YET, MOONLIGHT STILL SHONE
ON HER SKIN, WHICH GLOWED SOFTLY
AMIDST THE GLOOM.

the scene at the beach. Marie sat alone in the backseat as the sheriff drove her to the town's small emergency care facility. She leaned over and peered through a window covered in rings of dark mildew to search for the moon's familiar pocked surface, but couldn't find it, since the night clouds obscured the heavens entirely.

And yet, moonlight still shone on her skin, which glowed softly amidst the gloom. When she sat back, she met and held the sheriff's gaze in the rearview. The cruiser slowed, then stopped as he gazed at her radiant reflection.

"Take me away from here," she said.

The police cruiser turned away from the station. Instead, it drove on the road out of town, which led, eventually, to the highway, and then the unknowing world beyond. ●

MISSED CONNECTIONS #22:
GWEN AND THE ART OF ARCHERY

Words by Joel Preston Smith

Artwork by Brianna Spencer

was the guy who came in with his friend to get a compound bow restrung. He's not really my friend in a close and personal way. I say this just in case he has a bad reputation in your store, not because I immensely dislike him or he repels me vehemently or anything. We mainly just do sports together because we're also in some of the same classes where I go to college.

I don't mean to sound paranoid, but I noticed he talks a lot and asks a lot of questions that seem to wear down the other helpful sales associate and manhandles the more expensive (not that they're not worth every penny) and delicate items with gears and pulleys but mostly just buys economy bottles of bug spray and Weather-Tough camo sticks and you looked up the instant we came in and just as fast you were gone.

But not before I saw how beautiful you are.

I'm going to say something deeply personal and revealing as a kind of sign of faith and trust so you know how sincere and serious I am. Whew! Here goes: I have never really gone in for women with armpit hair and muscle shirts torn off at the midriff, but when I saw you hanging the imitation medieval crossbow on the pegboard behind the sales counter I thought the sun rose and set on your mohawk. This is when I realized that for most of my life I've had some kind of visceral aversion to strong, independent women. And that was revealing. Especially women that seem to defy every social norm or rail against what (I now see as) our patriarchal and puritanical American weltanschauung (1), that I would have blindly defined as "appropriate" or "decent" (2 and see also 13).

No longer. (3)

How bad was it? You didn't come back for five hours, so I knew it couldn't just be a smoke break. I had to tell my 'friend' to go back to the dorm without me. I told him I wanted to look around a while, and I did. I hung out by the carabiners and the tree perch thing for shooting deer in the back but Blake got kind of suspicious, like maybe I was a shoplifter or something. He kept coming over and offering help whenever someone wasn't up at the command post asking directions on how to taxidermy an elk or how to get the salt taste out of pemmican, and eventually we found out we have several things in common (4).

I suppose I kept staring up at the platform (here I go again building trust by confiding heartfelt emotions) fantasizing about how you'd look up there in your Army Ranger surplus cutoffs and canvas jump boots, so Blake asks me would I like to see how safe and stable it was and how everything looks from a commanding and tactical position (5).

When we came down I felt like a changed person. Not suddenly and entirely, but sort of subtly and stealthily and progressively. I asked him to show me some arrows and he did. We went over the basics and before I knew it I was buying things. At first it was just the Factor Z5 compound bow with the 35-inch axle and Shock Rod dampers (6) but then it was the

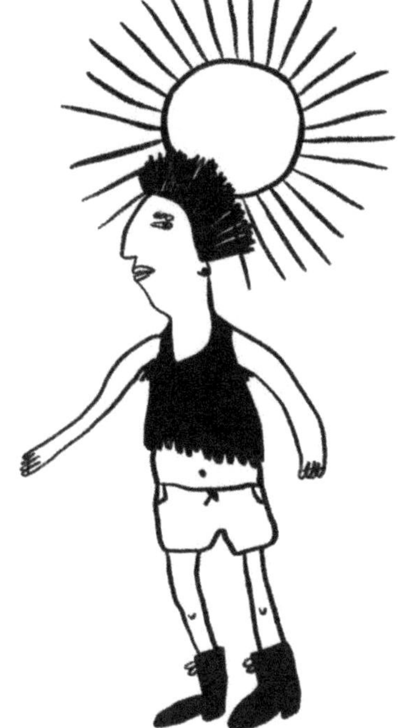

Cabella's Top-Loading Pack in winter camo with internal frame suspension and since I had that, I knew I'd need a 4-season 2-or-3 person tent with BiteAway® mosquito netting and Hyperlite™ Rain Fly and an 8-ounce bottle of leakproof BugsOff! atomizer for when I wasn't in the Areogel™ tent with my new Gerber Big Rock 9-Inch Camp Knife With Serrated Blade skinning something, or chewing into submission my new alpaca-leather laces for my new musk ox (7) suede boots with the VaporLite® copolymerized slip-resistant waffleboard soles to get the corral-vine fiber tanning scent out, which led of course to a magnesium fire-starter kit and a DIY pamphlet on bow drills in case the magnesium turned out to be carborundum (8), and there seemed no point to having all that without something to shoot, so I got some arrows, too.

But you never came back.

I would really love to see you. I feel I've started down a new path in a dark forest and I don't want to go down at it without at least talking to you first. I also forgot to get a sleeping bag. I don't know where to begin. Can a person learn on their own? Should I join a club? There's one (I think I mentioned) next to my school, but is the instructor any good? Do you have a list of qualified instructors? Are you on that list? If that list is full could I get on the waiting list? If there's no waiting list, would you be willing to start one?

I see that there's a Raw Foods Meetup and you're on that, and also the Portland's Women Hiking Group and Aboriginal Skills and Bushcrafting and Build Your Own Kayak and Environmental Balance and Harmony in Nature and Urban Foragers and Yarn Bombing.

I get all my raw foods at Safeway, so I'm good there, and Women's Hiking is out at least for the present moment (see below) until I take Advanced Rhetoric (haha), but I've almost always wanted to build my own kayak. I registered for Learn to Swim as a sign of good faith. Would you mind if came to Build Your Own Kayak? I already bought a hatchet, being an optimist at heart. Maybe we could talk there, before or after?

Reply with Foolish Mistake Number 9 that beginning archers always fatally make (22) so I know you're not just someone I don't want to build a kayak with. You can put just "M#9" in the subject line. Not that I'm trying to tell YOU what to do. You can put in any relevant thing you want.

Hope to hear from you soon at your earliest convenience.

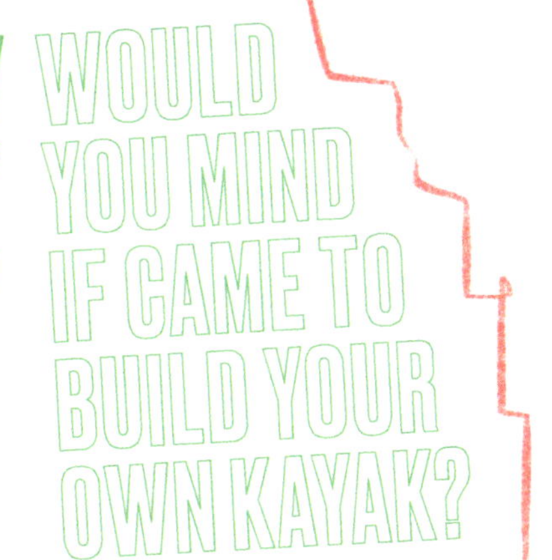

Footnotes:

(1) I started to explain that poofy term but then I realized you may very well speak fluent German (it somehow seems likely) or could very well have an advanced degree in cultural anthropology/industrial psychology. For me (a man, not dating at the moment) to assume that you (an archery expert, and the other guy says you also have a purple belt in Aikido) need ME, uninvited and unasked, to assume the hierarchical and patriarchal role of teacher/instructor is just laughable and inherently sexist and possibly suicidal. I am trying to get past these kinds of assumptions, I cannot possibly emphasize enough.

(2) I want you to know I don't subscribe to the so-called indisputable and independently reproducible and verifiable scientific studies that "prove" a predilection for violence and a preference for domestic beer over common tapwater is encoded in male DNA. That seems like nothing more than a gene-mediated Twinkie defense (9) to me. An outright evasion of the whole Nature vs. Nurture thing if I may put it so boldly. I don't think people should get off the hook simply by pointing a finger at their birth gender. Like "Dude, my junk made me do it."

If that were true, and scientific studies could be proven to show that women enjoy cooking, does that mean women should do ALL the cooking? It never seems to amaze me how much modern science gets misused to shackle certain oppressed masses to certain archaic and oppressive socioeconomic roles. What if I tell people I don't mind doing the dishes? AT ALL. Especially when it's something that hasn't been baked. Does that mean I'm gay (like FLAMING) or I obviously must be undergoing testosterone-reduction therapy or at least contemplating it? Obviously not, otherwise I would not ask you out for coffee and/or target lessons as soon as you see this. Which obviously calls those so-called 'verifiable' university-based studies into question (see 10 and see also 12).

(3) I almost said, "No longer, BABY," which just goes to show how embedded in the unconscious this patriarchy thing really is. It's even in our language. I think Hollywood probably also has a lot to do with it. In fact, if you really looked into it, I bet a lot of it (11) can be traced to the films of Humphrey Bogart and Francis Truffaut and staged monochromatic breakups in foggy European airports. I might do my junior thesis on this as we have a renowned cinema expert on the school faculty.

(4) Things Blake and I have in common that might surprise both of us: (a) mild acrophobia (b) tinnitus © !$@! autocorrect (d) the irrational but compelling belief that a green acorn carried in one's left pocket will bring spontaneous good luck (e) spicy Thai (f) failure to complete the novel Infinite Jest in just one sitting or ever

(5) What is it about being in high places surrounded by man's most dangerous inventions that makes you immediately think of humanity everywhere, black and white, rich and poor, red and yellow, the wide world over, who have ever grievously wronged you?

(6) Do you know of any cases where a person lets go of the bow part first instead of the string? Are there forensics reports on it? It's not in the 'Fatal List of 9' (see below) and my guess (after one try) is that that's an omission.

(7) Blake assures me these things are raised humanely. Cage-free, grass-fed, etc.

(8) Blake also explained your problem with the unreliable Chinese shipments (and that if it's not 98% pure magnesium I am due a full refund). He also suggested a poncho and a 6-pack of Sterno.

(9) https://en.wikipedia.org/wiki/Twinkie_defense

(10) Maybe it's just their methodology. I'm not alleging any personal abridgment of research ethics on the part of the (mostly privileged White male) principal investigators. And, to somewhat belabor the obvious point, just because mascara has been proven (12) to reduce the incidence of some kinds of skin cancers, does that mean women have to wear so much of it?

(11) "It." The only truly gender neutral pronoun in the entire lexicon, and I doubt it was out of benevolent social intentions from the blokes who dictate the Oxford English Dictionary.

(12) "Maybelline doesn't bat an eye at lacrimal litiginous melanoma," Mark Geddes, Randy Tramlion et al, Good Housekeeping, v.22, pg. 7, Mar. 20, 2003.

(13) It occurs to me that you might just be

IT OCCURS TO ME THAT YOU MIGHT JUST BE DRESSING (14) FOR WORK, AS IT WERE.

dressing (14) for work, as it were. That you might be an entirely different person outside Archer's Emporium. In fact, there might be some kind of regimented and obligatory dress code imposed by the oligarchical management and you're just doing your best to honor or submit to it (not willingly, I have no doubt). In that case I should do some backpedaling and point out that I also have nothing against floral cotton skirts or exquisite French perfume. I'm just against (almost militantly, which concerns me) the idea that just because someone could kill an intruder with her ring finger or thumb she can't also be tender, vulnerable and feminine.

Man! Yet another trap of patriarchy. You have to like just one thing or the other (not just as individual catalog-ish-type items but as entire categories of likables/contemptibles) and bitch like all get out to all your friends about the OTHER thing you are required by these primitive cultural conventions to despise and want nothing to do with for as long as you live, so !^#!ing help you God, so everyone in your kinship group and Youth Fellowship group and Eagle Scout reunion and Extreme Orienteering Meetup and Classic Car Collectors' Club and the all-inclusive gender-differentiation-obsessed culture at large knows which side of the genital fence you've got both balls of your feet firmly planted on. And it (15) just sickens me

(14) Caught another one. This one is even more subtle and insidious than "cooking." It's "dressing." Notice the "dress" part, the 'root' part—from Middle French, meaning "to direct, hence to arrange, to dress, hence also … to train a horse" (Partridge, 1958). "Dress" (I think it's safe to say) is a term meant to be applied (universally, I think it's safe to say) to the draperage of ANY human body past the age of birth, female OR male, via textiles (16) of assorted materials & manufacturing standards in

deference or obedience to religious or social or cultural mores, guard against abrasions, signify class, tribe or sect or social standing, or just keep the hell warm. NONE of which obviously has anything to do with dictating why women have to look ridiculous in hardhats.

(15) To no end.

(16) Not excluding synthetics, hemp and leather.

(17) Unless I were lesbian, of course, but trapped in a man's body. (18)

(18) It occurs to me that it is entirely possible I am a lesbian trapped in a man's body. I have to call my mother. (19)

(19) I have been disowned by my father. The inheritance. The two-story French colonial overlooking Fort Sumpter, where we spent every summer till I hit puberty and the guy who invented Coppertone bought the mansion next door. I'm talking about a Japanese ceremonial tea set here, hand thrown by none other than Master Iko Iia, who studied under legendary Sen No Rikū, latter half of the Ming Dynasty, 16th Century or thereabouts. Worth a small fortune if you also have the craquelure porcelain cosy, and we do. Everything. All of it. And my father has uninvited me (20) from a duck hunting expedition on the Outer Banks over spring break and to tell you the truth I didn't really want to go anyway.

I tried to explain to my 78-year old father that all my life I've preferred women to men but he just went berserk and told me I should have told him earlier and then maybe we could have done something about it because it's probably covered on his health plan, and how my silence was a sign of "failed trust" and that he was giving my Remington over-and-under to my

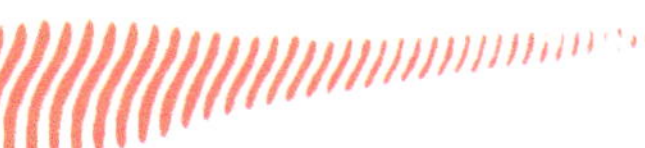
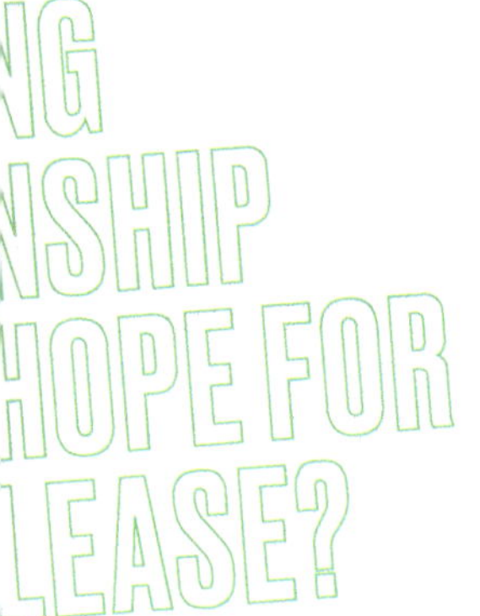
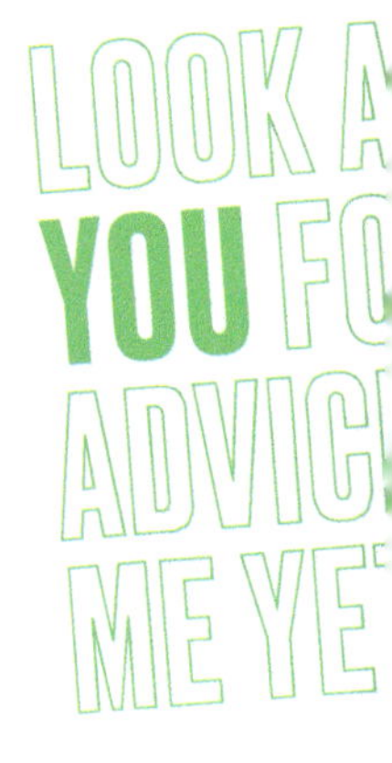

LOOK AT ME, ASKING YOU FOR RELATIONSHIP ADVICE! THERE'S HOPE FOR ME YET, RIGHT? PLEASE?

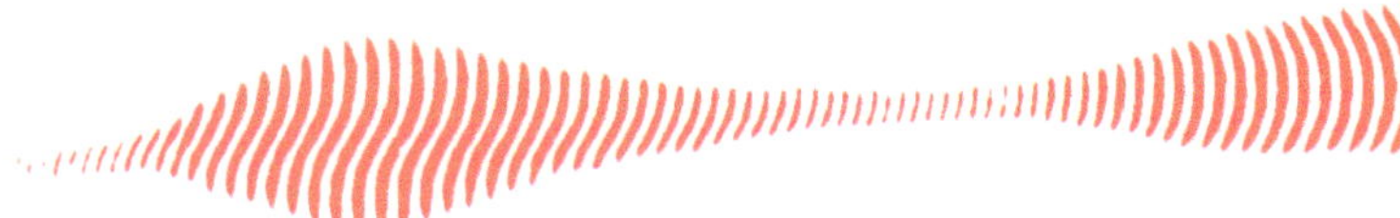

little sister, since I obviously wouldn't want or need it anymore. She's always been his favorite anyway (and I haven't shot anything in waders since I was 13). Whenever he needs to rehash his glory days firing artillery into random hillsides in Vietnam, it's her he emails. I don't know what to do about Christmas, or if that's even still on (for me, that is). God, I hate to say this, but maybe it's the optimist part of me that wants to know if he gets me something unisex, is that a gesture of reconciliation? What if he just FedEx's it (21)?

(20) This was not an "explicit" un-invitation. What my father said was, "Boy, I'matellya, you say 'at shit 'roun' the fellas and you DAMN well know you're li'ble tuh catch uh stray." It was said idiomatically in a regional dialect, but I think we both get the gist.

(21) Look at me, asking YOU for relationship advice! There's hope for me yet, right? Please? Maybe a long walk, if coffee is not your thing? Somewhere where we can talk, but also has steep inclines?

(22) That's another thing Blake and I have in common I forgot to mention: lists of things that could get us killed. ◐

HONOR ROLL

Raechel Wolfe

Billy Rancher And The Unreal Gods

Marshal McLuhan

Emma Luthy

X-Ray Café

Dorothy McCullough Lee

Dave Tracy

Karen Finley

Charlie Moses

Two Louie's Magazine

Raquel Divar

Help

Bud Clark

Ruben Allen

Lily Breshears

Lew Welch

Ret Marut

Hattie Redmond

Joni Renee Whitworth

Dr. Marie Equi and the 1913 Portland Free Speech Fight

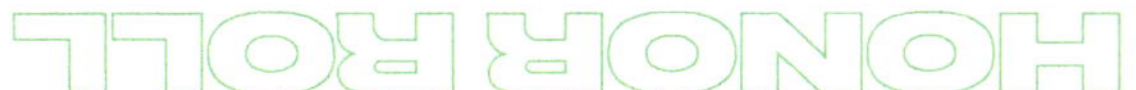

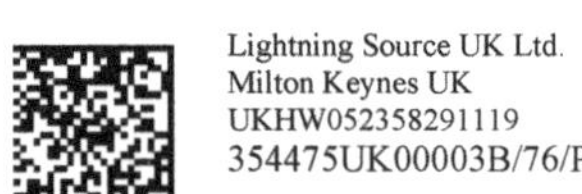

Lightning Source UK Ltd.
Milton Keynes UK
UKHW052358291119
354475UK00003B/76/P